Anita Zátori

Tourist experience co-creation and management

KT-378-614

LAP LAMBERT Academic Publishing

Impressum / Imprint

Bibliografische Information der Deutschen Nationalbibliothek: Die Deutsche Nationalbibliothek verzeichnet diese Publikation in der Deutschen Nationalbibliografie; detaillierte bibliografische Daten sind im Internet über http://dnb.d-nb.de abrufbar.

Alle in diesem Buch genannten Marken und Produktnamen unterliegen warenzeichen-, marken- oder patentrechtlichem Schutz bzw. sind Warenzeichen oder eingetragene Warenzeichen der jeweiligen Inhaber. Die Wiedergabe von Marken, Produktnamen, Gebrauchsnamen, Handelsnamen, Warenbezeichnungen u.s.w. in diesem Werk berechtigt auch ohne besondere Kennzeichnung nicht zu der Annahme, dass solche Namen im Sinne der Warenzeichen- und Markenschutzgesetzgebung als frei zu betrachten wären und daher von jedermann benutzt werden dürften.

Bibliographic information published by the Deutsche Nationalbibliothek: The Deutsche Nationalbibliothek lists this publication in the Deutsche Nationalbibliografie; detailed bibliographic data are available in the Internet at http://dnb.d-nb.de.

Any brand names and product names mentioned in this book are subject to trademark, brand or patent protection and are trademarks or registered trademarks of their respective holders. The use of brand names, product names, common names, trade names, product descriptions etc. even without a particular marking in this work is in no way to be construed to mean that such names may be regarded as unrestricted in respect of trademark and brand protection legislation and could thus be used by anyone.

Coverbild / Cover image: www.ingimage.com

Verlag / Publisher:
LAP LAMBERT Academic Publishing
ist ein Imprint der / is a trademark of
OmniScriptum GmbH & Co. KG
Heinrich-Böcking-Str. 6-8, 66121 Saarbrücken, Deutschland / Germany
Email: info@lap-publishing.com

Herstellung: siehe letzte Seite /
Printed at: see last page
ISBN: 978-3-659-68517-0

Zugl. / Approved by: Budapest, Corvinus University of Budapest, 2013

Copyright © 2015 OmniScriptum GmbH & Co. KG
Alle Rechte vorbehalten. / All rights reserved. Saarbrücken 2015

TABLE OF CONTENTS

LIST OF FIGURES

LIST OF TABLES

ACKNOWLEDGEMENTS

First and foremost I would like to thank my supervisor, László Puczkó, for his professional help, valuable advice and support during these years. I would also like to thank Ilona Papp, my first supervisor, who inspired me to take this long road of challenges. I am grateful to my colleagues at the Department who have watched over my work and supported me from start to finish. Furthermore, I am thankful to the professors at the Doctoral School for widening my methodological and theoretical knowledge, especially József Berács for his valuable comments and for lending me all those books. Gábor Nagy and Vakhal Péter were extremely helpful and always ready to answer my questions regarding statistical analysis. I am grateful to my Swedish colleagues at Kalmar's Linneaus University - especially my interim consultant, Bertil Hulten – for lending a helping hand in the literature review.

I am also grateful to Melanie Smith, Ivette Sziva and Noémi Kulcsár for expressing their professional opinions, and Rosemary Black and Stewart Clegg for their useful comments.

I would like to express my gratitude to all the tour providers who were open to taking part in the research - without their help and cooperation, this thesis would not have been possible.

Last not least, I am eternally grateful to my parents for their love and support, my dear friend, Judit Holp, for the encouragement and professional advice, and my partner Bálint Kodaj for his patience and valuable help.

The greatest experience for a human being is getting to know itself. Experiencing the world is intriguing, useful, beutiful, frighetning or illuminating; while experiencing who we really are is the greatest voyage, the most frighetning discovery, the most enlightening encounter. Being in Rome or on the North Pole is not as fascinating as learning something about ourselves, about the real nature of our character, about the way we relate to the world, good and bad, humankind, and passions. If my conscience is ready for such an experience, that is the only experience I seek.

Sándor Márai: Herbario (1943)

1. INTRODUCTION

The Sándor Márai quote in the motto adequately reflects the significance of experiences in the individual's life. Positive experiences contribute to one's psychological well-being, and most of these experiences manifest themselves in the form of the individual's leisure activities (Csíkszentmihályi, 1975). From the consumer's standpoint, tourism is a leisure activity and a source of memorable experiences. Csíkszentmihályi's study reveals that the most uplifting experiences are rooted in activities resulting in complete absorption and requiring the application of high-level creativity – which is referred to as the state of "flow". Márai's words also suggest that the writer regards travelling as a widely-accepted means of experience-generating activities.

Experience is the cornerstone of tourism, its alpha and omega. Tourism consumer experience comes to life simultaneously with the intention to travel in the form of anticipated experiences, which later influence the perception of the experience. After leaving the destination, the experience is not yet over, and lives on in the form of souvenirs, photos, and acquired habits and activities (e.g. a ceremonial dance, a recipe). It is also stored as a memory in the human brain, and appears as a narrative. Over time, external factors (such as campaigns, others' stories) might distort these memories, and internal factors might reevaluate them; while later on, past experiences can be the sources of new anticipated experiences.

Tourism is the market of tourist experiences – which sounds commonplace as is, but in January 2011, during my part-time PhD scholarship in Sweden, when I was first introduced to the concept of customer experience marketing and the experience-centric perspective, I felt enlightened, and these new theories shed an entirely different light on the system of tourism.

Throughout my doctoral studies, I have mostly focused on tourism marketing and destination marketing, thus the experience-centric approach is applied in this context.

The dissertation was prepared and submitted in two phases: the literature review and the research plan was submitted in March 2012, and in approved by the doctoral committee in June 2012. The preparation and realization of the primary research was followed afterwards, which ended in ended in September 2013.

Although tourists create their experiences according to their very own interests, as well as their social and cultural backgrounds, the business of tourism makes a significant contribution in giving life to a context for the aforementioned experiences, and what is most important: it influences – stimulates or hinders – the involvement of the tourist into a given experience.

This thesis examines the experiences rooted in tourist allures which also are the most determining factors regarding the overall destination experience. Consequently, the subjects of the research are destination experience mediators – tour providers offering city sightseeing tours for visitors. I chose Budapest as the location of my research.

The sample consisted of the managements, guides and customers (tourists) of the destination experience mediators.

One of my main goals was to explore the means of experience-creation conjured from the interaction between provider and consumer, thus the research examines the experience-creation of the consumer from the viewpoint of the provider.

I have also aimed to collect and process the experiences and know-how of tourism service providers putting the experience-centric approach, more precisely the staged experience concept and the experience co-creation concept into practice, while also examining the effects of latter concepts on the consumer experience.

The research was realized with the aid of the following research questions and their corresponding assumptions and hypotheses.

Question 1: How and to what extent does the experience-centric approach – particularly the staged experience concept and the experience co-creation concept – determine the management approach and service provision of tour providers?

In relation to the first research question, the following assumptions were determined:

- **Assumption 1:** The experience-centric approach is mostly characteristic of small-scale tour providers.
- **Assumption 2:** In the case of alternative tour providers, the experience co-creation concept is the ruling principle.
- **Assumption 3:** The staged experience concept is not predominant among any of the tour providers.

Question 2: How tour providers influence the consumer experience created during the tour?

In relation to the second research question, the following assumptions were made:

- H1: Interaction contributes to the degree of the consumer's involvement into a given experience.
- H2: The experience environment contributes to the involvement into a given experience.
- H3: Perceived customization contributes to the involvement into a given experience.
- H4: Involvement into a given experience affects the memorability of that experience.
- H5: Involvement into a given experience affects the authenticity of that experience.

Comparing the results of the two research questions, the following hypotheses are examined:

- H6: Tour providers preferring the experience-centric approach are able to reach a higher degree of involvement regarding the role of the tourist in experience-creation than providers preferring the non-experience-centric approach.
- H7: Tour providers mainly preferring the experience co-creation concept have the most success in involving the tourist into the process of experience-creation.

Figure 1: A methodological summary of the research

Source: own compilation (2013)

Figure 1 demonstrates a summary of the methodology used during the course of the research: in-depth, descriptive, and cause-effect researches were carried out based on the managements, employees, and consumers of the tour providers included in the sample.

The chosen topic and the magnitude of the research are primarily justified by the under-researched state and actuality of the topic, and the practical relevance of the research, as researchers of the topics highlight it. The empirical investigation of experience-centric management in the field of tourism is not explored thoroughly in international context, and it represents an empirically almost untouched area in domestic context. Tourist experience has been examined from the sixties almost only from consumer perspective. Tourist experience management theory has started to be formed and conceptualized from the new millennium only, since the publishing of The Experience Economy concept by Pine and Gilmore (1998, 1999), which drove the attention of academics to this aspect.

Experience management perspective is not uniform, and it is full of positivist management literature, offering best practices for business competitiveness and success. Lately the attention of the industry has turned towards how consumers are co-creating value and their experiences together with the company, brand and/or other consumers. This has also appeared in scientific investigations, mostly in area of general marketing. The importance of the topic was also articulated in circles of tourism academics.

The fact that the thesis lies largely on international literature also proves the novelty of the topic, because of the lack of Hungarian literature. From this reason, I had to create new Hungarian mutation and phrases based on the English one.

1.3. The structure of the thesis

In the first theoretical chapter of the thesis – namely, in **Chapter 2** –, I describe the importance of the consumer experience perspective, from both a scientific and a practical aspect. First and foremost, I analyze the theoretical foundations of the consumer experience, consequently pointing out the development of the concept from the 80s until present days, and define the concept. As a next step, consumer trends related to experience-seeking are investigated. In the last part of the chapter, I describe the features of „old", „new" and „newest" tourists.

Chapter 3 focuses on the conceptualization of tourist experience. It analyzes the development of the academic literature, the nature, definitions, complexity and influencing factors of the consumer experience, as well as those of memorable touristic experiences. The chapter interprets the tourist experience and its aspects from a business point of view.

Chapter 4 concentrates on the professional literature of tourist experience-management and marketing. The chapter defines experience co-creation and the concept of staged experiences. It discusses the experience-centric perspective related to tourism destinations. As an outcome of the literature review, a conceptual frame is created – defining the modes and aspects of the experience-centric management perspective. The literature review of the thesis follows the theoretical structure shown in Figure 2.

Chapter 5 provides an overview of the research question, hypothesis and methodology. It introduces the methodology of the research, and briefly describes the logic of the empirical part.

Chapter 6 introduces the methodology of the qualitative research, and the process of data collection adjusted to the chronological order of the steps of the research, **Chapter 7** focuses on the presentation of quantitative methodology. As a crucial part of the chosen quantitative research, it also describes the process of the related scale development.

Chapter 8 analyzes the results of the qualitative research. Applying the triangulation method, the data was collected through interviews, observations and questionnaire, and analyzed based on the conceptual frame established earlier. The related assumptions are answered at the end of the chapter.

The quantitative results are discussed in **Chapter 9.** These results are analyzed from the aspects of the hypothesis (structural) model.

Chapter 10 aims to conclude the results of the research. The qualitative and quantitative results of the two central research questions are discussed, and comprehensive hypotheses (H6 and H7) are evaluated. The main results of the research are highlighted and summarized.

Chapter 11 is the summary that evaluates the results from the aspects of theoretical, methodological and practical relevance, furthermore, it highlights the issues of validity, reliability and generalizability, and gives details on the boundaries of the research and future possible researches.

Figure 2: Themes framing the theoretical part of the thesis

Source: own compilation (2013)

2. CUSTOMER EXPERIENCE CONCEPT

Whether we turn on the television, read the magazines, or just go out for a walk, we are inundated by advertisements promoting products that promise to provide us with some new experience that is better, bigger, more genuine, or more fun than anything we have encountered previously. At the same time, consumers themselves are increasingly willing to go to greater lengths to experience something new or special. Experiences are not just added values of products or services anymore, but valuable goods themselves. "Customers are longing for experiences derived from the consumption of products and services, not for obtaining a product or service" (Puczkó, 2009: 25).

Sundbo (2009) divides the sectors of experience economy to two types – primary and secondary experience sectors. Primary experience sector refers to companies, which production is focusing on experiences. Business activities such as organization of festivals, producing movies, computer games, clothes, majority of tourism services belong here. However, according to Pine and Gilmore (1999) companies from any sectors are able of experience creation, and can apply the method of experience management. This latter is what Sundbo defines as secondary experience sector.

2.1. The theory of consumer experience

The experience is gaining more important role as success factor of company offers. The academic and managerial literature of customer experience has developed quickly, while the major part of it aims to explore and define the concept from theoretical perspective. Empirical research exploring the manifestation of the consumer experience concept applied by companies and service providers, is quite rare.

The concept of customer experience has appeared in the eighties contradicting the mainstream literature in consumer behavior (which deemed customers as rational decision makers), while the new experiential approach offered an original view to consumer behavior (Holbrook and Hirschmann, 1982). Holbrook and Hirschmann (1982) emphasizes the role of emotions in customer behavior, and the fact that consumers are sensitive and emotional beings, too, besides of being rational thinkers. **Despite of this, the customer experience perspective became widespread only at the end of the nineties, with the concept of experience economy.** Pine and Gilmore (1999) view experiences a new economic offers, following the evolution of economic value of commodities – goods – services. This brought a start of a flourishing time period for customer experience concept, and increasingly more publications has appeared focusing on this concept. Many of these had rather an advisory profile, but some academics contributed to the customer experience literature, as well (e.g. Addis and Holbrook, 2001, Caru and Cova, 2003, LaSalle and Britton, 2003, Milligan and Smith, 2002, Prahalad and Ramaswamy, 2004, Schmitt, 1999, Schmitt, 2003, Shaw and Ivens, 2005, Smith and Wheeler, 2002).

The base of these publications is a renewed way to consider the well-known concept of consumption – it defines consumption as a holistic experience which involves a person – as opposed to a customer – and interaction between a person and a firm, or a firm's offer (LaSalle and Britton, 2003). This approach points out the it is not the memorability of staged experiences and events what is of primary importance, but what contributes to the creation of value is the quality of the interaction between consumer and company (LaSalle and Britton, 2003), or as Prahalad and Ramaswamy (2004) put it: the co-creation experience. In this view, companies do not sell or stage experiences, but rather they provide contexts that support the experience creation of the consumer to enable them to co-create their own, unique experiences (Caru and Cova, 2003, 2007).

According to Schmitt (1999) the role of marketing is to create an optimal environment to support the customer experience. Moving from the basic idea of "engagement at different levels" he proposes a modular conceptualization of the concept of Customer Experience, which identifies five Strategic Experiential Modules:

1. sensory experiences (sense);
2. affective experiences (feel);
3. creative cognitive experiences (think);
4. physical experiences, behaviors and lifestyle (act); and
5. social experiences that result from relating to a reference group or culture (relate).

Gentile et al. (2007) differentiate six components of customer experience: (1) sensorial component, (2) emotional component, (3) cognitive component, (4) pragmatic component, (5) lifestyle component, and (6) relational component.

In their book Consuming Experience (2007) Caru and Cova identify a 'continuum of consuming experience' ranging from experiences that are mainly constructed by the customers to experiences that are mostly developed by companies (staged experiences), and in the middle are co-created experiences by consumers and companies (Prahalad and Ramaswamy, 2004, discussed in Chapter 4).

Based on the literature review of the major contributions, it can be stated that it is diverse, therefore various interpretations and conceptualizations of customer experience do exist. Despite the differences some common core characteristics can be identified: the customer experience has a personal and temporary character, and it involves and engages the customer in consumption at different modes: at rational, emotional, sensorial, physical, spiritual level.

2.1. Defining the experience

Experience is a complex term and phenomena, which can be conceptualized and described on various ways, and it counts as an important concept in different fields, such as psychology, sociology or business studies. Due to what its literature review is extremely rich and diverse. This justify why mostly business related definitions are collected and overviewed is this part of the thesis, however business related literature also takes into account the sociological and psychological perspective. The interpretative frames of the experience concept are:

- The **psychological perspective** builds the definitions of experience around personal feelings, memorability, consciousness and behavior.
- In case of the **organizational perspective**, the consumer, marketing, value and value creation concepts are in focus.
- The **sociological perspective** builds on sociological contexts such as lifestyle.

Defining of experience from psychological perspective:

At the most general level experience can be defined as "a continuous process of doing and undergoing that provides meaning to the individual" (Boswijk et al., 2005:2). Holbrook and Hirschman (1982: 132) indicate that experiences reflect an emotional state, consisting of "a steady flow of fantasies, feelings and fun." This resonates with similarity to the work of Csikszentmihalyi (1988), Holyfield (1999), and Gobe et al. (2001).

Kotler et al. (2001) also suggest that an experience for individuals comprises an emotional or internal condition. Pine and Gilmore (1998) indicates that experiences are of personal character, existing only in the mind of an individual who has been engaged on an emotional, physical, intellectual, or even spiritual level.

Experiences interrupt people from their lives and expectations to provide something of interest that demands attention; experiences themselves are highly involving (Ray,

2008). According to Carlson (1997) an experience can be defined as a constant flow of thoughts and feelings that occur during moments of consciousness.

The definition of experience based on organizational perspective:

According to Hirschman and Holbrook (1982) experiences are those facets of consumer behavior that relate to the multi-sensory, fantasy and emotive aspects of one's experience with products. However it is also interpreted as a blend of many elements coming together and involve the consumer emotionally, physically, intellectually and spiritually (Mossberg, 2007). Based on O'Sullivan and Spangler (1998) the experience involves the participation and involvement of the individual in the consumption and the state of being physically, mentally, emotionally, socially, or spiritually engaged found that experience

An alternate definition is provided by La Salle and Britton (2003: 38), who see that an experience which has value is: „a product or service that when combined with its surrounding experiences events goes beyond itself to enhance or bring value to a customer's life. This is the ideal – to deliver such overall value that a product transcends the ordinary to become extraordinary or even priceless." This sometimes means moving into the backstage of experience delivery (see MacCannell, 1973).

From a consumers perspective experiences are enjoyable, engaging and memorable encounters for the consumers (Oh et al., 2007). In Lewis and Chambers' (2000) view the total outcome to the customer from the combination of environment, goods, and services purchased.

Pine and Gilmore (1999: 11) define experience from an organizational/business sense. For these writers an experience is created when "a company intentionally uses services as the stage and goods as props, to engage individual customers in a way that creates a memorable event."

According to Gentile et al. (2007) the customer experience derives from the interaction between a customer and a product, a company, which provoke reaction, while the experiences is strictly personal, and implies the customer's involvement at different levels (rational, emotional, sensorial, physical and spiritual).

Definitions based on sociological perspective:

Based on Schmitt (1999: 25) experiences are: „the result of encountering, undergoing or living through situations. …triggered stimulations to the senses, the heart, and the mind. …connect the company and the brand to the customer's lifestyle and place individual customer actions and the purchase occasion in a broader social context.

…experiences provide sensory, emotional, cognitive, behavioral and relational values that replace functional values"

The experience is a primary article of the tourism industry, which justifies the investigation of the customer experience perspective in field of tourism. However, it is assumed that in business practice the concept of customer experience has not been applied broadly, because of the lack of unified terminology, theoretical models, and management tools and methods.

Before the literature overview of tourist experience theory (see Chapter 3), I would like to present the context and factors, namely the customer trends, which has contributed to the wider recognition and application of this concept.

2.3. Consumer experiences in the light of global and tourist trends

Which factors have affected consumer behavior during the last few decades? What are their consequences, and how do they appear? In the followings, global and tourist trends will be revealed, alongside with their consequences having an effect on the growing importance of consumer experiences. According to Prahalad and Ramaswamy (2004a), the changing role of the consumer is the most significant factor: the isolated consumer is now full of connections, the unknowing became well-informed, and the passive one became active. This is also supported by ETC (European Travel Commission, 2006) which pointed out the recent changes in lifestyle and experience-seeking as the main trends in tourism.

2.3.1. The impact of changing lifestyle

Experience is placed on the top of Maslow's hierarchy of needs (Maslow, 1970). They are essential for the existence of a welfare state, therefore, as the welfare increases, so does the social demand for experience.

Based on people's *attitude towards leisure time and work,* from industrial times to ours, there are *three different stages* (Krippendorf, 1986). Even though travelling and leisure-time activities are essential parts of our lives today that has not always been the case.

The first stage is the stage of *"live to work"*, which was typical during the industrial era. The motivation for travelling is rather limited for those who live to work (Poon, 1993): revitalization, recreation, rest, being served, relaxation, being free of problems, chores, and duties.

The second stage is the stage of *"work to live"*, which is a feature of the lifestyle of the post-industrial society. Leisure-time activities are a part of everyday life, while the motivations to travel are (Poon, 1993): to experience something different, exploration, need for change, entertainment, pleasure, and game, to be active, togetherness, stress-free rest, free will, to get closer to the environment.

Those who experience the *new unity of everyday life* belong to the third stage, the ones who aim to reduce the difference between work and leisure time. They look for fulfillment in all areas of life – good working and living conditions and a vivid life are important for them. The motivations to travel for those who belong to said stage are: to widen their breadth of view, to learn something new, to get closer to their inner selves, to encourage communication with others, experiencing the simplicity of life and the environment, to become creative and open-minded, experimenting and taking individual risks (Poon, 1993).

Based on the assumptions, the representatives of the second stage are the most widespread in the developed countries; however, the characteristics of the first two lifestyles fade with time. According to Krippendorf (1986), by the 21th century, the third stage will be the most dominant.

Uriely (2005) has stated that the understanding of the differences between work and leisure time become blurred. O'Dell (2005) points out the loosening of the borders between tourism, leisure time and work, too. Moreover, Urry (1990) and Lash and Urry (1994) directed attention towards the connection between tourist experiences and everyday experiences in their postmodern works published in the '90s. Ryan (2002) observes that more and more workplaces provide areas for leisure time activities, such as gyms or spas. Ryan and Birks (2002, in Uriely 2005) write about working tourists' involvement in leisure-time activities while on a business trip, such as visiting relatives and attending sports events. Puczkó (2009) describes the methods of working while travelling, which is more and more common due to the development of modern technology.

One of the most crucial elements is undoubtedly the spreading of the internet and its fast development. The revolution of communication technologies allows the flow of ideas and information, and decentralizes them from the companies (Fisher and Smith, 2011). **The content and the brand are no longer written by the companies,** but by the consumers and their communities. The consumers became 'writers' and the new technologies made communication between consumers and firms bi-directional, providing more interactivity (Fisher and Smith, 2011). Due to this process, consumers gain more and more control over creating offers (Lusch et al., 2006). Consumer content now has nearly as much influence as paid commercials.

More and more consumers become active, well-informed and rich in connections. They analyze and understand the offers on the market before making the decision to purchase something; they have increasingly more information available to decide which companies they would like to connect with. **They no longer depend only on the communication with the company itself**. Their opportunities for sharing information and advice keep increasing due to the rising importance of social media.

Prahalad and Ramaswamy (2004a) believe that the advance of the internet and technological development result in changes which can be examined from different aspects:

- *Information access.* People are much more informed due to the enormous amount of information available. This phenomenon has the biggest effect on those sectors that previously lacked extensive information sharing (e.g.: healthcare, finance). For example patients under medical treatment can now collect information online about their symptoms or illness, taking a more active role in influencing the curing process.
- *Global view.* Consumers can now reach any part of the planet thanks to the internet. They are not limited by the range of products available in their location; they can compare prices and choose from a variety of other offers before buying the desired item.
- *Networking.* People are drawn by their natural desire to gather around common interests, needs and experiences. The spread of the internet and mobile technologies support the formation of consumer communities. Their power is hidden in their independency from the companies, so the reliability of their opinion is high when discussing consumer experiences.

- *Experimenting.* Consumers have the opportunity to experiment with product development, especially in the case of digital products. While consumers share their experiences online concerning all aspects (e.g.: recipes, gardening advice), they learn from each other's observations; which creates a whole base of knowledge accessible to anyone, anytime.

2.3.3. Rising consumer activity and experience

The customer desires to be an active participant rather than a passive consumer. Based on her observations from the tourism market, Auliana Pool already stated in 1993 that consumers become more and more active. Morgan cites Suvantola (2002) who said that tourists do not simply encounter the physical space of a destination but construct their own experiential space from it according to their motivations and interpretations. Many of the experiences offered by tourism, e.g. the physical challenge of adventure and activity, the sensual delights of gastronomy or wine tasting, the intellectual discovery of arts and cultural events or even the excitement of shopping, involve skilled consumption (Scitovsky, 1976) or serious leisure (Stebbins, 1992, 2007; in Morgan et al., 2009). By this is meant that participants gain increased satisfaction through continued improvement of the capabilities, skills and knowledge required for the activity.

The ETC study (2006) shows that by the tourists visiting more places, **they become more experienced**, their need for new travel experience grows. Increasingly more people demand **constant flow of new experiences,** and when visiting a destination they look for **deeper, more significant experiences**.

The development of information technologies is contributing to the growing trend of consumer activity. Prahalad and Ramaswamy (2004b) state that the more relevant information reaches an individual, the more experienced they become. Therefore they are able to make more personalized decisions, and they also wish to customize the service or product, and take a more active role in consumption.

Authenticity, meaning genuineness, is a central concept in contemporary consumption (Arnold and Price, 2000). Authenticity can be interpreted in several ways:

- First of all, *objective authenticity*, which is related to the authentic origins of the offer (Wang, 1999).
- On the other hand, authenticity can also be a result of consumption. Wang (1999) calls it *constructive authenticity*, when authenticity is defined in a symbolic manner, reflecting a personal evaluation.
- Wang defines a third type of authenticity: *existential authenticity*. Opposed to constructive authenticity, existential authenticity is not defined through the personal, subjective evaluation of the authenticity of the product or the service, but it is formed by personal feelings arising during the act of consumption. This type of authenticity derives from the perception of (reaching) an authentic state of being.

Related to the definition of existential authenticity, Morgan (2010) questions the importance of authentic experience in tourism: is it possible that the consumer views the artificial environment through a ludic and ironic lens (created by the postmodern views), and by entering that specific atmosphere, they start to enjoy its overly artificial elements? This question refers to the relevance of the postmodern sociological perspective in tourism.

Based on the postmodernist views[1]:

- the post-tourist can be a tourist even at home (e.g. due to technology creating a virtual reality) (Feifer, 1985),
- for post-tourists, tourism is rather eclectic (Feifer 1985),
- post-tourists play[2] multiple games (Feifer 1985),
- post-tourists have hyper-realistic views (Eco, 1986),
- post-tourists accept tourism to be a mass-product (Rojek, 1993).

---

[1] Its representatives claim to be rather interpretators, than codifiers of the modernist views

[2] During the organised group sight-seeing tours, they take on the „role of children", they are told when to visit the bathroom, wen and where to eat etc. – those tourists, who experience sight-seeing as children, play that they are tourists (Urry, 1990).

The importance of signs has increased in the postmodern society, and became more important than the hidden content (Williams, 2006). **Hyper-reality** is a key term in postmodernism, pointing to the disappearance of the differences between real and unreal, while unreal starts to seem more real than real itself (Baudrillard, 1993, Ritzer and Liska, 1997). The popularity of virtual communities is a fine example for that phenomenon (Puczkó, 2009).

According to Fischer and Smith (2011) increasingly more companies try to please consumers by making **offers providing authentic consumption.** Today's consumer is seeking authentic experiences, while also aspiring to balance between the activities defined by the supplier of the experience and the ones defined by themselves, **leaving ground to improvisation, sense of freedom and self-expression** (Binkhorst and Dekker, 2009). The concept of value co-creation (Prahalad and Ramaswamy, 2004a) enables companies to engage consumers as co-creators and to customize their offers. More and more consumers *look for experience co-creation,* rather than supplier-created ones – choosing creative tourism or volunteer tourism, which can result in more meaningful experiences (ETC, 2006).

Overall, it can be stated that as a consequence of increasing individualism in developed countries, the demand for customized offers and consumption continue to intensify. At the same time, the understanding and the perception of authenticity widens. Both of these factors have an impact on influencing the experience-seeking behavior of consumers. The experience is personal and subjective in nature, which reasons why authenticity and personalization are two typical dimensions of it.

2.3.5. Consumer communities

Due to the new, interactive communication techniques, consumer communities tend to mobilize, and obtain a more significant role on the market. (Prahalad and Ramaswamy, 2000). Virtual space allows individuals to create global communities **around different activities, products or interests.** Those communities become centers of information for potential and recent consumers. The significance of consumer communities has already been acknowledged by marketers, therefore they try to affect their creation or operation. As a result, those communities today are believed to have a brand building role (Schau at al., 2009).

The communities are built around a favored product or brand. However, the new dominant paradigm (Vargo and Lusch, 2004) emphasized that the product itself is not an ending point, but rather a connection: sharing experiences and ideas between consumers. Consequently, the product may have a secondary role, while the main emphasis lies on **the interaction and sharing of experiences among community members.** The trend shows that **neotribes,** *new community interest-groups,* are becoming the primary source of information, knowledge, entertainment and security (ETC, 2006).

For the customer, the significance of a product is further increased if it transmits experiences (Prahalad and Ramaswamy, 2003). The formation of communities is not solely the privilege of the consumers. It is essential for companies to form unified networks to be able to create competitive experience offers (Fischer and Smith, 2011, Prahalad and Ramaswamy, 2004).

2.3.6. The old, the new and the newest tourist

Poon in her book, *Tourism, Technology and Competitive Strategies,* published in 1993, has created the term **new tourist,** based on the changes brought about by new consumer trends. The new tourist is an experienced traveler who has special interests due to his individualistic aims to have control over travelling, often makes spontaneous, unpredictable decisions concerning travelling, and for whom vacation does not mean escaping everyday life anymore, but making him richer. Moreover, the new tourist looks for an outstanding price-value ratio, appreciates what is different, and pays attention to not have a negative impact on the visited destination's environment or culture. Despite the fact that Poon (1993) has summarized her observations more than twenty years ago, her statements are just as valid today. She highlighted six characteristics of the new tourist which differs most from the ones of the old tourist:

- the new tourist is an experienced traveler,
- considers different values important,
- has a different lifestyle,
- is characterized by different demographic features,
- is flexible, and
- is a free-spirit.

A fact that must not be overlooked is that **old tourists** are still present on the market. The significance of the new tourists lies in their growing numbers among the consumers of tourism.

The **old tourists** (Poon, 1993) form a homogenous group, their consumer behavior is predictable, security is of high importance to them (which can be achieved e.g. by participating in organized group trips), travelling is something new for them (since they are less experienced travelers), they regard travelling as a way of escaping daily routine, the quality of service is less important for them, they are mainly interested in passive relaxation (like sunbathing), and they do not tend to consume services not included in the package (for example in Turkey's biggest seaside destination, in Antalya, only a fraction of the tourists accommodated in all-inclusive hotels visit the city center individually).

Mass tourism is another typical element when speaking of the old tourists. Mass tourism was described by Ritzer's and Liska's (1997) structuralist, modernist view entitled the 'McDonaldization of society', which declares that not only the economy, but society is also affected by the process of McDonaldization. The authors compare Disney parks to McDonald's, but also equal them to monumental cruises, theme parks, casinos, shopping malls etc. The modernist approach describes society through the view of the *grand narrative* as increasingly efficient, predictable, foreseeable, and led by technologies (Ritzer and Liska, 1997).

Based on the latest consumer trends, the characteristics of the new tourist is not the latest. Following the earlier terminology of Poon's, I refer to the group of tourists driven by the latest tourism trends as **the newest tourists**. The study of the ETC (2006) shows that by visiting more places, tourists become *more experienced*, they become more aware of the visited destination's environment and culture, while they reflect on their own previous experiences and lifestyle more often. The study further explains that *internal tourist experiences* become more significant (desire for self-improvement, demand for creative self-expression etc.), as opposed to external tourism features (such as demography, climate). As the tourist experiences of a traveler accumulate, it influences their desire to travel more; many of them become *carrier-travelers*, demanding constant flow of new experiences, and they seek a deeper, more meaningful experience during the visit. The ETC study warns that most travelers aim to get rid of the *tourist label* and experience destinations on their own. Experienced travelers master the aspects of the organization of a tour, therefore they expect travel agencies to provide higher quality service and additional values (ETC, 2006).

The characteristics of old, new and newest tourists are shown in Table 1.

Euro RSCG (2010) highlights some recent emerging trends of the travel market: flashpacking, geo-tourism, raw luxe, slow travel, staycation and voluntourism. *Flashpacking is* a trend set by stylish backpackers who tend to reside in cheaper accommodations (like hostels), but spend more on cultural and sport activities and gastronomy in the visited destination. *Geo-tourism* indicates travelers who care about the sustainable welfare of the area's environment, aesthetics, culture and local community. *Raw luxe* is a term for those tourists who purchase high quality service; however, they also look for authentic experiences which allow individual interpretation and self-improvement. *Slow travel* means experiencing the destination as a local, to purchase local goods and services, to connect with the location, its people, and its culture. Usually, it takes a longer amount of time (weeks, months) than average vacations. *Staycation* refers to a vacation spent at home or nearby, while *voluntourism* is a term for travelling with the aim of volunteering.

In conclusion, it can be stated that **the newest tourists** are at the most sophisticated level of experience-seeking; **new tourists** form a group with a constantly growing and deepening experience-seeking behavior; however, the consumer behavior of old tourists is also influenced by recent trends.

Table 1: The features of the old, new and newest tourist

Old Tourist	New Tourist	The Newest Tourist
Old tourists form a homogenous group, are predictable	Tends to make spontaneous, unpredictable decisions concerning travelling	spontaneous, unpredictable decisions concerning travelling, travelling is a part of their life, ,,global nomads"
Security is their key concern, which is ensured by organized group trips	As a result of individuality aims to have control over travelling	An individualist, experienced traveler, understands all aspects of organization, has full control over the tour
Travelling is a new experience (less experienced traveler)	Experienced traveler	Career-traveler
Travelling is a way of escaping the daily routine	Travelling means enrichment of life	Aims to get rid of the tourist label, and have a full-contact experience with the visited destination
The quality of services is important	Quality and value-price ratio is important	Seeks higher quality, satisfactory value-ratio and additional values
Desires passive relaxation (e.g.: sunbathing)	Active and experience-seeker (e.g.: hiking, cultural tourism)	Demands constant flow of new experiences, deeper, more meaningful experience while visiting a destination
Not likely to consume offers outside the obtained package	Has special interests	Desires to experience existential authenticity
Is less interested about local culture, does not care about his impact on local environment and society	Appreciates difference, pays attention not to have a negative impact on the environment or culture of the visited destination	More aware of the environmental and cultural values of the destination, and reflects more on his own past experiences and lifestyle.
External factors have bigger influence on the tourist motivation (demography, climate etc.)	External and internal motivational factors	Internal motivational factors (demand for self-development, demand for creative self-expression etc.)

Source: own editing based on: ETC (2006), Euro RSCG (2010), Poon (1993)

3. THE TOURIST EXPERIENCE

The central theme of the third chapter is the investigation of experience as a theoretical concept in tourism. Tourism is a primary sector of experience creation. Just as customer experience, tourist experience is a complex phenomenon, which is characterized with compound nature and can be interpreted on multiply ways. The current chapter introduces the development of tourist experience literature, the analysis of tourist experience's nature, complexity, and describes the process view of tourist experience. Lastly, the chapter ends with studying the most recent conceptual dimension of the topic – the memorable tourist experience.

3.1. The development of tourist experience literature

The tourist experience grew to be a key research issue in the 1960s (Uriely 2005), becoming popular in the social science literature by the 1970s (Quan & Wang 2004). At this time, the tourist experience was discussed by authors, such as MacCannell (1973) who related it to authenticity and Cohen (1979) who explored experience in terms of phenomenology.

A snapshot sampling of tourism related literature shows that tourist experiences and tourism experiences have been written about since the sixties when Clawson (1963) wrote about related recreation experiences and Boorstin (1964) commented on authenticity with regard to tourist experiences. Smith (1977) edited works focussed on host-guest interactions and experiences. In the eighties Feifer (1985) and Pearce (1982) extended traveller and tourist experiences discussions in association with authenticity and incorporated consideration of motivations. In their work Mannel and Iso-Ahola (1987) studies tourist experience from three perspectives: conceptual perspective, post-hoc satisfaction, indirect perspective.

In the nineties and beyond, Ryan (2002) produced edited works addressing the "tourist experience" with a number of linkages to motivation theories. Urry (1990) commented on authenticity and tourist experiences in addition to interpreting tourism experiences and tourist experiences using "tourist gaze".

From the 1990s, researchers started to use experience-based research approaches in an effort to develop a better understanding of the tourist experience, for example tourist reporting thoughts and feelings in diaries (Andereck et al. 2006).

In the 2000s, a number of conferences have dealt with the "experience" concepts – such as, *Measuring Experiences,* Travel and Tourism Research Association (2004); the *Extraordinary Experiences Conference* (2007); and *Tourist Experiences: Meanings, Motivations, Behaviors* (2009). From an industry perspective, tourism experiences and quality tourism experiences have become a continuously more used term in tourism and hospitality sectors.

The above overview cannot be claimed as very detailed or all-including, its aim was rather to highlight some main contributions to the tourism literature in the topic. Based on the literature review in the overview, it can be stated that experience concepts are present in the tourism literature for the past fifty years.

Ritchie and Hudson (2010) distinguished among the various levels/types of experiences that conceptually seemed to form an **evolutionary trail of experience thinking**. This trail involves the basic experience, the satisfactory experience, the quality experience, the extraordinary experience and the memorable experience (see Figure 3).

Figure 3: Evolution of researched experience dimensions

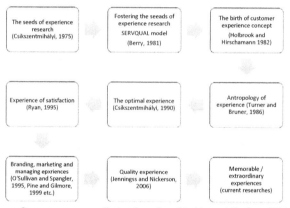

Source: own compilation based on Ritchie and Hudson (2010)

The framings of experiences have been described by Jennings et al. (2009) as (1) organizational / business-based, (2) individualistic, (3) psychological and (4) social in nature. Organizational-based framings focus on *marketing, value and delivery*; individualistic framings relate to *personal, affective, embodied and memory*; psychological framings were associated with *feelings, memory, intellect and behavior*; social framings were noted as connected with *lifestyle, and social contexts*.

Quan and Wang (2004) recognized two complex academic perspectives in the studies of tourism experience:

- **a social science approach** (e.g.: Cohen, 1979; Lee & Crompton, 1992; MacCannell, 1973, 1976; Urry, 1990) with a focus on the *peak touristic experience* as one of the main pull effect of visit, and as contrasted with the daily life experience, and
- **marketing/management approach** (e.g.: Moutinho, 1987; Swarbrooke & Horner, 1999) based on customer orientation, and integrating the *supporting consumer experiences* – derived from the activities facilitating the peak experience, such as transportation, hospitality.

Ritchie and Hudson (2010) differentiated **six broad categories / streams**, each of which appeared to reflect a stream of thinking and related research. The streams identified were as follows:

- the *fundamental stream* that involves conceptual work and/or research that sought to define and understand the *essence* of the tourism experience.
- a stream of thinking and research that aims to understand the tourist's experience-seeking *behavior*;
- a *methodology stream* that is related to specific methodologies applied in tourism experience research;
- a stream including those studies that sought to explore and understand the nature of *specific kinds of tourism/attraction experiences*;
- a stream that involves the *managerial* concerns related to designing and developing the tourism supply systems required to manage the delivery of the tourist experience;
- a stream aiming to distinguish among the various levels/types of experiences that conceptually seemed to form *an evolutionary trail* of experience thinking (basic experience, the satisfactory experience, the quality experience, the extraordinary experience and the memorable experience).

3.2. The complexity, nature and dimensions of the tourist experience

No single theory has been widely accepted to define the meaning and extent of tourist experience, although a number of authors have made attempts to formulate models by generalizing and aggregating information. Due to its complex nature, research in area of tourism experiences is challenging, having various manifestations.

In general marketing literature consumer experiences were studied in the last couple of decades. Hirschmann and Holbrook (1982) were the first to question the limitations of seeing consumer behavior solely in terms of cognitive information processing. According to them leisure experiences are subjective, emotional states laden with symbolic meaning, and consumption has hedonic as well as functional, utilitarian motives.

3.2.1. The nature of tourist experience

According to a consensus, consumer experience can be characterized as a **multidimensional but "holistic" evaluation** (e.g. Schmitt, 1999; Gentile et al., 2007). Different dimensions or factors form this holistic view, even if in some cases a certain person is only aware of them at subconscious level. The notion of explaining experiences in terms of a holistic concept is originating from a psychologist Max Wertheimer. According to this school of thought (Gestalt), the human mind works in ways that are holistic, parallel, and greater than the sum of its parts, so much of our individual perceptions and experiences are viewed holistically. Tsai (2005) differentiates two facets of consumer experiences: (1) a phenomenological level, of which consumers are fully aware, and (2) a cognitive level where transformation and learning happen.

Experiences are argued to be *subjective, intangible, continuous and highly personal phenomena* (O'Dell, 2005). In McIntosh and Siggs (2005) view tourism experience is *unique, emotionally charged*, and of high personal value. Based on Uriely (2005) tourist experience is currently depicted as an *obscure and diverse phenomenon*, which is mostly constituted by the individual consumer.

In Michalko and Ratz's (2005) view tourist experience can be various. Among the most typical one they include:

- excitement, adventure (e.g. lived experience from rafting),
- actual or perceived threats (such as survivor's tour),
- new knowledge and skills (such as knowledge acquired in a crafts camp),
- aesthetics (e.g. experience from a picturesque landscape),
- togetherness (such as a romantic honeymoon experience),
- novelty (e.g. experience from a new activity tried),
- exotic (experience created by learning about distant cultures).

Researchers, academics and professionals have defined the tourist experience on multiply ways, but what most of them agree on is the priority of consumer perspective. In majority of well-known academic tourism journals the terms of 'tourism experience' and 'tourist experience' occur with the same frequency, and mostly expressing the same definition and concept (Ritchie et al., 2011). While 'tourism experience' rather refer to an organizational view, 'tourist experience' rather refers to a consumer perspective.

At the most general level experience can be defined as "a continuous process of doing and undergoing that provides meaning to the individual" (Boswijk et al., 2005: 2). Experiences are highly personal, subjectively perceived, intangible, always fleeting and continuously on-going, nonetheless, as commodities they are more than randomly occurring phenomena located entirely in the minds of individuals (O'Dell, 2005). The tourist experience has been defined also as "the culmination of a given experience" formed by tourists "when they are visiting and spending time in a given tourists location" (Graefe & Vaske 1987). The tourist experience is "an example of hedonic consumption" (Go, 2005: 81), which "the tourist is seeking" (Volo, 2005: 205).

Based on Walls et al. (2011) the hospitality and tourism consumer experience is a **multidimensional** construct comprised of a number of **external and internal** factors that shape and influence consumer experiences, which can exist only if the participating consumer is willing and able to participate. Other define it as "a complex combination of factors that shape the tourist's feeling and attitude towards his or her visit" (Page et al. 2001: 412–413).

Accoding to Andersson (2007) tourist experience is a moment when tourist consumption and production meet. Lashley (2008) study and define tourist experience from the perspective of host and guest, and define it as emotionally engaging, which leads to memorability. However, Larsen (2007) defines tourist experience as a past personal travel-related event strong enough to have entered long-term memory.

To conclude, we suggest that until now there is no single theory that defines the meaning and extent of tourist experiences, although a number of authors have made attempts to formulate models. Based on various definitions tourist experience can be described as:

- having a **personal character**,

- **multidimensional construct** consisting of external and internal factors, which can exist only if
- the consumer is **able and ready to be involved** in the experience.

Quan and Wang (2004) suggested that tourists' experiences must be seen as an organic whole in which **peak** (art, culture, heritage and other tourist atraction) and **supporting experiences** (accommodations, transportations, shopping, entertainment establishments) complement each other. However, the dynamism of the market change the character of some tourism activities and open a whole new set of experiences (e.g. virtual reality).

It is important to highlight that experiences may have both positive and negative consequences, regardless of the intention towards the quality of the tourism experience. Moreover, positive and negative relationships with tourism experiences can be associated with the multiple interpretations of quality, which need to be *contextualized within temporal, social, cultural, political and environmental considerations* (Andereck et al. 2006).

As Volo (2009) notes it, experience is composed of all the events that occur between sensation (e.g. an observer's awareness of an energy form impinging on a receptor physiologically designed to transduce it) and perception (e.g. the interpretation of the sensation), as well as memory (e.g. the subsequent organization and recall of such interpretations). The human capacity of memory allows individuals to anticipate experiences, and the ability to categorize dissimilar things, allows them to sort anticipated experiences into those they might seek and those they would avoid.

Aho (2001) distinguishes four essential cores of tourism experiences: **emotional experiences, informative experiences, practice experiences, transformation experiences**. Some of these four core contents of tourist experiences appear in various degrees often simultaneously.

Another useful typology of experiences was introduced (Aho, 2001) referring to their character as having **physical, social or mental** contact with the subject. Tourists can have physical experiences in bathing and massage places, for instance. Social experiences are important in many types of travel, both in incentive tourism of active businessmen and more leisure tours for the elderly people. Mental experiences are common both in pilgrimages and in tourism devoted for art. Touristic motivations can be classified on the basis of these three basic categories of elements.

Cole and Scott (2004) proposed four stages of the tourist experience, namely: *dimensions of performance quality, dimension of experience quality, overall satisfaction, and revisit intentions.* Cutler and Carmichel (2010) set up a tourist experience conceptual model based on impacts and outcomes. In this model the tourist experience is all that happens during a tourist even (travel to site, on-site activity and return travel). The anticipatory phase and recollection phase are still presented, demonstrating how the tourist experience is planned and anticipated before a trip takes places and remembered after a trip has finished. During the experience three categories of influences are presented (based on Nickerson, 2006; and Mossberg, 2007), involving those elements outside the individual:

- *physical aspects* (involving spatial and place-based elements of the destination),
- *social aspects* (encompassing the various social influences on experience), and
- *the influence of products and services* (representing factors such as service quality, leisure activities or tourist-related products available).

The immediate **outcomes** of experiences are argued to be related to the overall evaluation of the trip, which can be judged through satisfaction / dissatisfaction (Ryan, 2002). This overall evaluation can affect and is affected by elements within the **personal realm**, such as *knowledge, memory, perception, emotion and self-identity.* Though these elements can be seen as outcomes, which can change and develop after an experience through reflection and recollection, they can be impacted by the experience itself. Moreover, these elements shape the experience, as tourists arrive at a destination with individual memories, perception of place and people, knowledge about the world and understandings of self (Ryan, 2003; Selstad, 2007). The personal realm then feeds into **motivations and expectations** for future experiences, providing a cycle of motivation / expectation, experience and outcome. That is how the cycle of motivation/expectation – experience – outcome is formed in Cutler and Carmichel's tourist experience model.

People vary a lot in their **personal resources** to receive experiences. Time and money are the most commonly mentioned resource types, but they are not the only important ones. Various personal resources contribute in different ways to the resource potential of experiences of people. The following list includes the most important types of personal experience resources (Aho, 2001):

- **time** for thinking, planning, anticipating, receiving and reflecting experiences,
- **money** for buying services needed for approaching and receiving experiences,

- **skills** of approaching and self-contributing to experiences,
- **attitudes** – openness towards new things and possible unexpected happenings,
- **knowledge** (including earlier experiences) background for finding information of, evaluating and choosing between available experiences,
- **social networks** for anticipation, delivery and sharing of experiences.

The overall resource potential of the subject is based on these six personal experience resource factors. The possession and use of various types of personal resource potential has influence on scope and strength of experiences.

Another approach shows that tourism experience can be categorized into **four dimensions** (Volo, 2009):

- *Accessibility dimension* (how accessible is the tourism experience to a potential consumer)
- *Affective transformation dimension* (what degree of affective transformation is experienced)
- *Convenience* (what level of effort is required to access the experience)
- *Value* (what is the benefit received per unit of cost)

Finally, the **variability** of the experience is another aspect to be considered, because different people may engage in various experiences (Volo, 2009; Uriely, 2005).

3.3.1. Interpretation of constructs from the perspective of the planned research

As the research questions of the thesis focus on business perspective of the tourist experience, the theory should be analyzed, which interprets and defines the service provider's impact on tourist experience, and the experience creation process. In Walls et al. (2011) model the firm is presented as an external influencing factor. Based on this model the tourist experience is a multidimensional construct, which consist different external and internal factors, in case the consumer is able and willing to participate in the experience creation. The authors built a model reflecting the influencing factors of an experience, based on Belk (1975), Bitner (1992), Hirschman and Holbrook (1982), Schmitt (1999), Schmitt and Simonson (1997) (Figure 4). Based on this conceptual model the core consumer experience is comprised of two axis indicating if the personal experience to what extent is ordinary or extraordinary, cognitive and/or emotive, meanwhile it highlights that all experiences are unique for each individual. The model also illustrates number of factors influencing the consumer experiences: perceived physical experience elements, human interaction elements, individual characteristics, and situational factors.

Figure 4: Factors influencing consumer experience

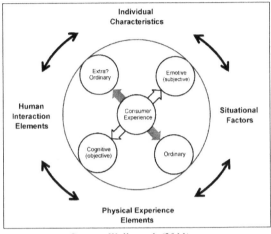

Source: Walls et al. (2011)

Part of the **environmental and physical experience** elements and interaction factors belongs under the firm's control. The physical and environmental experience factors can be viewed as experience environment. Businesses, in an effort to impact the consumer, stage and enhance the physical environment in order to appeal to the five senses of the consumer and create a physically appropriate environment that meets their marketing objectives. These elements may, for example, include items such as a smelling a flower scent when entering a hotel lobby, warm and welcoming color schemes, and a properly designed environment that is both practical and visually appealing. Destinations also affect the tourist experience through their experience environment formed by natural, cultural, sociological factors. The visitor, during his/her visit, gets to an interaction with service providers, locals, other tourists and so on. From all external impact factors, first of all it is the destination experience intermediates (Ooi, 2005) who influence the tourist experience, because these actors interpret the tourist attractions which form the core experiences (see Puczko and Ratz, 2000).

From the perspective of **human interaction factors** it is important to highlight the appearance and behavior of front line employees, and also the marketing management perspective of the firm – in what extent does is it allow the interaction between host and guest, and in what extent does is apply the experience-centric approach. The research aims to investigate these questions as well.

Individual characteristics, such as personality type, values and sensitivity to the environment, influence the individual's willingness or ability to recognize staged and co-created experience elements. **Situational factors in tourism** often influence the quality and nature of the trip. These factors include the purpose of trip, the weather, travel companions, and nature of destination, all of which support or not the traveler's willingness to recognize staged and unstaged experience elements. It is also important to highlight personal resources – e.g. time, money, skills, and knowledge – as internal factors which respond for the uniqueness of the experience. Although the research does not aim to study the internal factors, consumer survey is about to be realized which requires the acknowledgement of subjective nature of experience evaluation.

3.4. The process view of tourist experience

Most of the definitions of tourist experience refer to the experience in the destination; however, the experience of a tourism event begins before the trip: in the planning and preparation phases, and continues after the tourist returns through the recollection and communication of the events which took place.

Number of authors agree with the process view of tourist experience (see Aho, 2001; Borrie & Roggenbuck, 2001; Botterill & Crompton, 1996; Li, 2000). Using multiple phases to describe experience comes from leisure studies, which argue that leisure is a multi-phased event. The Clawson and Knetsch (1966) model involves five distinct yet interacting phases starting with anticipation, travel to site, on-site activity, return travel and recollection. Studies in tourism also indicate that experiences do change over time, demonstrating this multi-phase framing. Based on the unstable nature of tourist experience, Aho (2001) points out seven stages of the experience process:

(1) orientation (awaking interest to some degree),
(2) attachment (strengthening interest resulting in the buying decision),
(3) visiting (the actual visit consisting of travel to and staying in the destination),
(4) evaluation (comparisons with earlier experiences and alternatives, and conclusions for future actions,

(5) storing (physical – photos, films, souvenirs; social – people and social situations to remember; mental – affections, impressions and new meanings),

(6) reflection (repeated spontaneous and staged presentations of the experience,

(7) enrichment (presentations of films, souvenirs; arrangement of meetings and networks to cherish memories; new practices created during the trip).

These stages are linked into a dynamic system where previous stages are necessary, but not sufficient conditions of later stages. New experiences can emerge and old ones may be modified at each stage the experience process being thus cumulative in its basic character. Visiting, of course is assumed to be the core of influence.

Larsen (2007) also agrees with the process view, and distinguishes the following process phases: (1) the planning process (the individuals' foreseeing of tourist events through expectancies), (2) the actual undertaking of the trip (events during the trip), and finally (3) the individuals' remembering of these tourist events.

3.4.1. Business perspective interpretation

As next, the interpretation of the tourist experience's process type conceptualization from business perspective follows. From the process view models Aho's concept is applied, as considered to be the most detailed and significant.

As tourism is basically a voluntary activity, **orientation** in form of awakening interest to touristic experiences can be defined as a necessary starting point of the process leading to decisions of travel, and later to tourist experiences. Orientation and bonding can be influenced by the promotional activity of the service provider sector, marketing campaigns, and branding. Experience perspective has been applied in this field, too, and the message of the communication has moved from being product-focused towards being experience-focused. Destinations increasingly try to communicate the myth, the experience of the destination from which a visitor can take her/his part if s/he visits to the destination (see e.g. the Incredible India campaign).

The process of **visiting** is the arena for absorbing raw material for experiences; a part of it leads to immediate reactions, while a part may ripen over a longer time. During the visit a direct interaction is formed between the firm and the consumer. To what extent is the tourist able to get involved in the experience, to what extent is the service able to engage the consumer, is a crucial issue from the perspective of experience evaluation.

Evaluation of visits is usually made informally. Experiences are related to earlier trips and expectations. Service provider can influence the evaluation of the experience on various ways – directly, during communication with the customer after the visit (e.g. in email, social media), and indirectly, through marketing campaigns, as they also influence the re-evaluation of past experiences (see Braun-Latour, 2006).

The new experiences are related to the accumulated storage of one's earlier experiences and the existing image of others' experiences. Visits are commonly registered and taken with in various forms utilizing technology. Souvenirs and photos are the most common tools of making memories concrete. That is one of the reasons why a service provider or a destination should considerate the role, quality and variety of souvenirs. Moreover, if possible, it should point out recommended spots for photo shooting to enhance to tourist experience and its storing.

The **storing** of physical objects, however, is not the only significant way of storing visits. Also social features like interesting people and significant social situations may be stored. Mental affections, impressions and new meanings are commonly known results of tourist visits. Various written travel descriptions are a classical form of long-lasting storage on these rather abstract elements. The effect of a short moment's experience and last over centuries in a popular travel description – like that of Acerbi's from the year 1799 (Aho, 2001). Therefore, it is suggested that storing is a very significant stage in the process of experiences. It also represents the necessary basis for the two last stages of the process.

Reflection of experiences is both an indication of and a way of increasing their strength. These reflections may take place either privately or in social arenas. Most intimate experiences belong to the private sphere and their reflections are difficult to trace. However a large majority of tourist experiences offers interesting material for social communication: exceptionally good destinations are rewarded with praising comments offered to all kinds of people met soon afterwards. If a visitors' group has developed social community it may organize a meeting for seeing the pictures and reflecting the events during the visit. Reflections may be spontaneous or staged. They are based on the stored material of visits. The time, effort and frequency devoted to reflections may be considered as good proxies for the significance of the tourism experience.

In the process of experience **enrichment** existing social networks represent an essential personal resource. Anticipation of experiences is vitalized in hearance of stories told by friends and others having been to the potential destinations. The post-experiences of trips are vitalized in communications with and within various social networks of the subject.

The current primary research aims to investigate the tourism service providers' influence on the process of experience creation, in its whole length. While from consumer point of view, only the phase of visiting is being empirically studied.

Memory is an important dimension of the tourist experience (Larsen, 2007; Pine & Gilmore, 1999). Noy (2007) argues that tourism practices are the resources for experience, which are accessible only in the form of representations through memory. Memories can be defined as filtering mechanisms which link the experience to the emotional and perceptual outcomes of a tourist event (Oh et al., 2007).

Memories have an impact on the evaluation of tourist experience. Based on Oh et al. (2007) memories consist both cognitive and affective readiness of relevant information, both volitionally and involuntarily retrievable. According to them, memories also tend to be significant when tourist experiences are disappointing: negative destination experiences might lead to a vivid memory instilling a negative attitude toward the destination. Therefore, it can be stated that memories are likely to act as an important filtering mechanism, because they **link the experience to other attitudinal outcomes** of the tourist experience.

Pine and Gilmore (1999; Gilmore and Pine 2002a, 2002b) suggested that a **well-staged** experience will shape the tourist's attitude toward the destination in a positive manner, and it leads to enhanced memory. Accordingly, a well-staged experience leads to positive memories, which in turn shape tourists' subsequent attitudinal evaluations, such as overall satisfaction and future intentions (Pine and Gilmore 1999; Oh et al. 2007). They argued for practical strategies of offering tourists motifs or memorabilia with an aim to create vivid memories about the destination experience. At the heart of engineering Pine and Gilmore's **four realms** of experience, therefore, is the creation of positive memories; fostering a memorable experience is essential to a destination's ability to provide the four realms of experience (for more see Chapter 4).

The importance of memory as an influential aspect of experience is also highlighted by Selstad (2007) and Cary (2004). Though memory is seen as the outcome of experience, it can also be actively involved in the interpretation and transformation of experience through **narration** (Selstad, 2007). The narration of memory allows experiences to change, indicating that experiences are not stable in nature; they can continually evolve and change. Tourists are involved in the production of meaning of the destination experiences (Selstad, 2007). Cary (2004) reiterates this argument, stating that **there are differences between actual experiences and the later representation of experiences in narratives**. In taking a cognitive approach to the study of tourist experience, one must consider the mental memory processes, as this memory will be all that remains after the experience has ended (Larsen, 2007). Therefore, it can be argued that memory is the most influential aspect of tourist experiences.

Different factors set the memorability of events, such as affective feelings, cognitive evaluations, or novelty of the events. Kim et al. (2010) developed **a Tourism Memory Scale**, according to which seven constructs – **hedonism, refreshment, local culture, meaningfulness, knowledge, involvement, and novelty** – are important components of the tourist experience that are likely to affect a person's memory.

The memory is a crucial deputy in recognizing tourist experiences, it allows individuals to **anticipate experiences** (Volo, 2009), and to sort anticipated experiences into those they might seek and those they would avoid.

Memories may be **enhanced by the presence of sensorial experiences**, as emotional events appealing to the senses tend to be remembered better than non-emotional events (Dolcos and Cabeza, 2002). Kim et al. (2010) call for research that compares travelers' memories and future intentions at each stage of the experience, such as anticipation, on-site, and recollection, from the reason to provide valuable information to destination marketers. Aho (2001), based on the process view of tourism experience, suggests that **experiences should be studied at their latest stage**, after their evaluation and enrichment; and Larsen (2007) defines tourist experience as a past personal travel-related event strong enough to have entered long-term memory.

Wirtz et al. (2003) found that tourists' predicted affects during the tourist trip were significantly stronger than the on-site negative- and positive effects, moreover that tourists' level of expected negative and positive affect were significantly higher than the on-site negative and positive affect reported by the same individuals while on tour. The research results revealed that **the remembered experience from a tourist trip is the one that best predicts the tourists' desire to repeat that current experience.** The best predictor of the subjects' wish to repeat the holiday, indeed the only predictor, was remembered experience. Remembered experience was however strongly related to on-site (real time) experience, although there were very weak and insignificant paths between on-site experiences and the wish to repeat the experience. These results indicate that on-line experience, what happens while on tour, or while at the destination, does not predict tourists' desires to repeat or not repeat a tourist trip. It is what people remember that predicts this. In addition, **these results indicate t**hat the best predictor of the desire to repeat a trip is memories of the trip, i.e. retrospective global evaluations, and that such memories are superior in predicting peoples' future choices.

Braun-Latour's (2006) study led to three interesting findings about the formulation of post-experiences. First, post-experience information, whether received in advertising or through word-of-mouth memory stories, can influence and even distort how a tourist remembers his or her past. Second, that not only does this false information change the consumers' own personal memory of their visit, but it can change their overall knowledge structure (semantic memory) for the target destination. Third, that more presentations of false information lead to greater false memory creation than if that information is presented only one time. Despite the results, Braun-Latour (2006) concur with past researchers that tourists will attempt to rely on their past experience with a destination when they make future decisions.

Regarding **peak and end effect of affective experiences** Fredrickson (2000) highlights that such experiences are evaluated by just a few selected moments, namely the peak and the end. Several studies indicate that evaluations of past affective experiences, as well as decisions about the future, can be well-predicted by a simple average of these two moments, i.e. the most affective moment (the peak experience) of the event and the affect experienced at the end of the event (the end experience). One interesting consequence of this is that the duration of the event hardly carries any weight at all. Fredrickson asks why this is so – and suggests that peaks and ends are carriers of subjective meaning – understood as information that contributes to the individual's understanding of him/her-self vis-a`-vis the world around the individual (it is in other words not merely the serial positioning effect of recency that account for this end-effect).

Wright (2010) acknowledges another way of exploring the everyday consumption of past leisure and tourism experiences: the importance of Clawson's post-trip reflections by looking specifically at **how we attach personal meaning** to our socially constructed memories. The author is highlighting two reflexive memory-based methodologies, both of which can be used to explore lived experiences through the construction and consumption of personal narratives. The first, Memory-work, is a feminist-inspired framework created by German socialists during the early 1980s

(Crawford et al, 1992; Onyx & Small, 2001). The second is Autoethnography. Chaim Noy applied the technic of autoethnography while researching personal tourist experience.

In his Autoethnography of poetic tourist, Noy (2007: 350) reveals his belief that *"when people recall and recount their tourist-related experiences, they take on the expression of re-calling a dream, a daydream or a (religious) vision. They seem to be focusing on a point that lies elsewhere, beyond or past the here-and-nows of everyday spaces and routine practices"*. The similarities between Noy's results and the existence of a 'third space' discussed by memory workers such as Small (2008) appear to emphasis the complexity of (re)interpreting the meanings attached to past experiences. Again, like Small, Noy also comments about the correspondence and increasing overlapping relationship between tourism and everyday life. He acknowledges and appears to support Urry's view **that people in modern society are tourists for much of the time**, whether it is merely a case of recalling the past, experiencing the present or dreaming about the future (Urry, 1990).

Morgan and Pritchard (2005) attempt to look at how the tourism experience can influence our behavior and identity (both self and social). In their opinion, tourism studies and research should attempt to reflect the discourse of transformation and the self-consciousness of the 'tourist moment', because tourism is a part of our everyday life. Furthermore, Wright (2010) highlights that while tourism has been traditionally seen as a means of escaping the everyday, our post-trip recollections are inadvertently situated within our daily lived environment.

The literature review of memorable tourist experience was useful, as it represents an experience dimension, which is a central topic of recent empirical researches (see Figure 3). Besides, memorability of tourist experience, as a variable, appears in the research plan of the thesis. During the analyzes of the nature, complexity, impact factors, process view, and memorability of tourist experience, the aim was to realize a comprehensive literature review of the aspects of tourist experience – especially those related to the empirical part. As a next step, different concepts of experience-centric management approach will be investigated.

Tourism is essentially a marketplace of experiences, and tourists provide the mental frames where the tourist experience happens (Volo, 2009). Tourism is a pioneering example of the experience economy as evidenced in earlier literature from the 1970s (e.g., MacCannell 1976; Cohen 1979), and as Sternberg (1997: 952, 954) succinctly put, "tourism primarily sells a 'staged' experience... tourism's central productive activity [is] the creation of the touristic experience."

Management writers and consultants applying the experience concept offer different advices and approaches for business transformation (e.g. Schmitt, 1999, 2003; Shaw & Ivens, 2005). In contrast, few academic authors have taken up research into the managerial as opposed to the behavioral, sociological and psychological aspects of the consumer experience paradigm (Morgan, 2010).

More recently, Prahalad and Ramaswamy (2004) have called for a strategic approach, allowing customers to co-create their own experiences in search for personal growth. The emphasis thus shifted in recent debates from narrow notions of staging or production to broader conceptions of experience creation, involving a wider range of agencies and processes (Sundbo, 2009).

Caru and Cova's work, Consumer Experience was published in 2007. The authors apply a systematic view on experience and value creation between the company and the customer, and form a model called Continuum of consuming experiences (Figure 5). At the one extreme are experience created alone with the consumer, at the other extreme are experiences of which creation a company had a major effect, between the two extremes, in the middle, are co-created experiences. The role and marketing approach of the company differs in these three cases:

- in case of individual experience creation the company or service provider typically applying traditional and product oriented marketing strategy,
- in case of staged experience creation the company / service provider plans and realizes the experience in a very detailed way, which enable the consumer to immerse to the consumption and experience,
- in case of experience co-creation the company / service provider attempt to create an optimal experience environment in which the consumer can create his/her experience.

Figure 5: Continuum of consuming experience

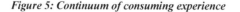

individually constructed experiences co-created experiences **staged / developed experiences**

Source: own compilation based on Caru and Cova (2007)

The two extremes of the continuum describes the participation mode of the consumer in experience creation. In case of experiences which are mainly constructed by consumers, the level of consumer activity is high, in case of staged experience creation the level of consumer activity is enough to be low due to his/her passive role.

At one of the extreme experiences that are mainly constructed by consumers may involve company-provided products or services. The consumers form their experience, while businesses in this case does not aim to prioritize the experience creation process. The consumers based on their own abilities give real value (cultural, symbolic, and functional type) to ordinary objects or services. It is suggested that the notion of appropriation should be introduced (Filser, 2002; Ladwein, 2002; Cova and Dalli, 2009). Acts of appropriation are the mark of a fundamental psychological system of action that transforms and personalizes the experience. According this phenomenon, consumers provide competencies in effort to become the main builders and co-creators of the consumption experience (Holt, 1995), and that they engage imaginatively, creatively, and constructively with the world around them (Sherry Jr et al., 2007).

At the other extreme, we find experiences that companies have largely developed or staged, and in which consumers are immersed in a context that is usually hyperreal (Cova and Dalli, 2009). Pine and Gilmore (1999) suggest to deal with hyperreal, company-managed experiential consumption, and the involvement of consumers into the experience.

In the middle of the continuum we can locate experiences that have been co-created by companies and consumers, during the interaction process between them.

In the next subchapter Pine and Gilmore's experience economy perspective and the concept of staged experience will be discussed, followed by the co-created experience type, where Prahalad and Ramaswamy's value co-creation concept gets to the focus, which emphasizes the importance of experience co-creation.

The experience economy concept is closely related to tourism both in its origins and its implications (Morgan et al. 2009). Pine and Gilmore's (1999) assertion that the developed world was moving from a service- to an experience-based economy was based partly on their analysis of the growth of US leisure and tourism attractions. It is interesting that Alvin Toffler (1970) futures studies researcher already 30 years before Pine and Gilmore pointed out the paradigm change which will influence the business. He described this new wave of paradigm as experience economies.

In Pine and Gilmore's (1999) definition experiences are distinct economic offerings that are as different from services, as services are from goods. In their view, successful experiences are those that the customer finds unique, memorable and sustainable over time, would want to repeat and build upon, and enthusiastically promotes via word of mouth. Experience management concept highlights the importance of customers and their experience (not of products and services) in the business process. The concept aims to create competitiveness by focusing on the improvement of customer experience through experience engineering.

The experience economy perspective highlights the important role of staged experiences as sources of added value (Pine and Gilmore 1998, 1999, Gilmore and Pine 2002a, 2002b, Boswijk et al. 2007). Higher level of consumer experiences enhance satisfaction, while for the company the increased value will be reflected in higher income, due to increased sales and/or prices.

According to the staged experience perspective the understanding of the value customers place on experience should be designed into the company's brand as the basis for its competitive strategy.

Pine and Gilmore (1999) have applied the drama concept of Goffman (1959) into the management theory, based on their view the drama concept should be placed to the center of business strategies. The experience economy and the concept of staged experience adopt drama terminology, so from customer service personnel become actors, from customers become audience, from physical environment will be settings, and the service becomes a performance or show. The drama concept was already adopted in variety of consumption-related contexts, including consumer experience (Holbrook and Hirshman, 1982) and services (Grove & Fisk, 1989; Grove et al., 1992). But Pine and Gilmore go beyond this by using the metaphor 'work is theatre' when describing business sectors focusing on creation of staged experiences.

Morgan et al. (2008) argues about servicescapes formed by businesses, and describes it through personal drama and interaction taking place in a dining room. They describe how the tourist often becomes the — or one of the — actor(s) on stage in the show and the manager's role becomes one of providing the space in which the experience is co-created. The supplier can provide the tourist with a scene, with other actors, but it is the customer's mood and state of mind, her reactions to — and interaction with — people and events that make an experience (Csikszentmihalyi, 1990; Pine & Gilmore, 1999; Anderson, 2007; Morgan et al., 2009). It is the individual ability and need to participate, relate and co-create in these circumstances.

Morgan et al. (2009) identified a number of key recommendations which are derived from the 'work is theatre' metaphor:
- the importance of the setting, the design and ambience of the service environment or servicescape (Bitner, 1992; Pine and Gilmore, 1999);
- the importance of staff / customer interaction (Berry et al, 1985; Gronroos, 1985; Grove et al., 1992);
- the need for staff to put something of their personality into their roles (Pine and Gilmore, 1999);
- an emphasis on charting and scripting each stage of the service encounter, often using metaphors from drama and storytelling (Grove et al., 1992; Pine and Gilmore, 1999; Schmitt, 2003; Shaw – Ivens, 2005);
- a view of service delivery as an integrated production in the cinematic (continuity management) rather than the factory sense of the word (i.e. a concern that each time the customer encounters the brand they should get the same high-quality experience) (Pine and Gilmore, 1999; Schmitt, 1999, 2003; Shaw, 2005; Smith and Wheeler, 2002).

Pine and Gilmore (1999) see experience management as a strategic tool, as well as, an operational one. The drama is perceived as the interaction between the company and its customers that creates the experience. Those service providers can create the biggest value who are able to support the consumer's personal development.

Pine and Gilmore (1999) identify **four realms** of experience (Figure 6), which are differentiated in terms of the level of customer involvement and participation. The four dimensions are entertainment, education, esthetics, and escapism. The entertainment and esthetics dimensions are described by passive participation, when the consumer does not influence the outcome of the service. In contrast, education and escapism dimensions involve active participation wherein consumers play a key part in the process. Active participants will personally affect the outcome of the service, as they become part of it.

Figure 6: The four realm model of experience

Source: adopted from Pine and Gilmore (1999) and Oh et al. (2007)

The tourist typically *absorbs* entertaining and educational offerings of a destination and *immerses* in the destination environment resulting in esthetic or escapist experiences. Absorption here is defined as "occupying a person's attention by bringing the experience into the mind" and immersion as "becoming physically (or virtually) a part of the experience itself" (Pine and Gilmore 1999, p. 31).

According to the authors each of the four dimensions ultimately combine to form a so-called *sweet spot*, which is the optimal consumer experience.

Those experiences we think of as **entertainment**; such as going to a show, usually involve customers participating in a passive manner. Based on Williams (2006), for tourism service providers however, the key to this realm may be to apply it more holistically, and to incorporate entertainment into areas outside of the immediate experience.

In the realm of **education** participants usually acquire new skills or increase those they already have, e.g. surfing or learning salsa. Many tourism offerings include educational dimensions; such as informal lectures, guides or background information. The potential exists for further increasing the "educational" element of many tourism and hospitality offers (Williams, 2006).

The escapist dimension includes activities in need for active participation and immersion. Sport activities performed during travelling – such as biking, skiing are typical examples. However, the dimension itself is much broader in other activities – such as having a mind-opening conversation, singing karaoke with locals etc.

The **esthetic** experiences are passive in nature. The participants are immersed in the activity, but have little effect on its environment, such as looking natural beauty of Meteoras during the tour, or indulging in a coastal sunset. Much tourism activity is of an esthetic nature, with tourists immersing themselves in the experience, but with little active participation in the experience – this dimension is the most crucial realm of tourist experience. According to Pine and Gilmore (1999) the esthetic realm involves a more intense experience than the entertainment experience.

Petkus (2002) tries to simplify the understanding of these dimensions, and capture the essence of each realm. He suggests that the entertainment realm involves sensing, the educational realm learning, the escapist realm doing, and the esthetic realm being there.

Most of the academics in tourism accept the four-realm model (Williams 2006; Oh et al. 2007; Hosany & Witham 2009) or accept it with some objections (Morgan et al. 2009; Ritchie & Hudson 2009). However the model has not been fully underpinned empirically yet. Oh et al. (2007) made the first empirical test by implementing the experience economy concepts (including the four-realm model) into tourism. They developed a valid scale, but neither the American bed and breakfast industry research (Oh et al., 2007), nor Hosany & Witham's research about cruiser's experiences (2009) confirmed the model explicitly. In both cases the esthetic dimension was the only significant determinant of experiential outcomes (like arousal, memory, overall perceived quality, satisfaction, and intention to recommend). This was also supported by results of a primary data collection realized by me in Sunny Beach, Bulgaria in August 2011. Mehmetoglu and Engen (2011) tested the four realm model in context of a Norwegian music festival and a museum. The results showed that in case of the music festival only the realm of escapism, in case of the museum only the realm of education supported the customer satisfaction. This might lead to a conclusion that **the four realms do not equally contribute to the outcome of an experience.**

According to Pine and Gilmore's hypothesis (1999), only by creating unique and memorable experiences for its consumers can any business achieve a lasting competitive advantage, and in context of tourism this carries a particular relevance to tourist destinations (King, 2002; Williams, 2006).

The experience in the context of destinations is closely related to the creation of myths, which Stamboulis and Skayannis (2003:40) define as „an organized, designed experience and an accompanying narrative". The myth of the destination is known for the tourists beforehand, and becomes a reason for their choice of destination. As the tourist experience has a continuity character (Aho, 2001), myth also has one. While staying in the destination, guests expect to live the myth, and after they leave, the myth lives on in their memory. Such a myth can be expressed as an experience-based brand story, a well-known phenomenon and tool in marketing. According to Stamboulis and Skayannis it is obvious that this requires close cooperation between the tour operator and the local community. The experience-centric management assumes active participation and involvement of the tourist, and the participation of local communities on tourist experience creation at destination level (Stamboulis and Skayannis, 2003). Every involved member from the local community takes out his/her part from, and slip to the role just as the destination would be a theatre.

The importance of customer communities gathering around a destination (and destination brand) should be also acknowledged. Destinations may achieve the creation of a consumer community in spontaneous way or by direct or indirect encouragement. In a more developed form, a consumer community or more communities may connect to a destination, which will function as a reference point for them.

Experience themes are articulated in destinations as collective social artifacts, which involve both planned and spontaneous elements. The tourist can immerse in it, and can actively participate in it. The interaction between **place, theme and tourist** is the main source of knowledge creation. Only a knowledge creating process is able to produce this type of new, innovative, and complex process. „The creation of experience texts on specific myths presupposes the accumulation of detailed information about tourist tastes, preferences and values" (Stamboulis & Skayannis, 2003:41). The success of narratives depends on the capability to deal with the information collected through ICTs and experience, through DMO and supplier intelligence.

Destination myths and stories created socially are not limited in space or time. The consumer might continue to interact with it after she has departed. The reproduction of the experience may cause the extension of the host (destination) – guest interaction, and vice versa. Communities might be formed around the destination brand, but destinations also can support their formulation. Stamboulis and Skayannis (2003) advise to destination to interact directly with consumers, because only this can lead to a successful creation of experience themes.

In academic circles the emphasis has shifted from narrow conceptions of staging or production to broader notions of experience creation, involving a wider range of agencies and processes (Sundbo, 2009).

The four realm model can be criticized from many perspectives. It might be questioned if it covers all the realms and tourism activities? Aho (2001) states that the four-realm model does not cover all relevant types of experiences in tourism. For example, cure (getting healthier) and various types of personal achievements (e.g. activities resulting in self-satisfaction) are not covered. As it was argued previously, empirical studies neither did confirm the four realm model.

Pine and Gilmore (1999) illustrated their concept with the success of Disneyland and other themed parks. However, the overuse of Disney-like cases led to the ideas of the experience economy being superficial and dismissed, moreover, rather product-centered than customer-centered (Morgan, 2010). Ritzer et al. (1997) distinguish authentic spaces from simulated environments, and criticize as inauthentic the experience-management emphasis on staging performances. Nijs (2003) criticizes the staged experience approach. She argues that in more feminine European cultures, the experience needs to be grounded in the social and environmental values of the company. For the creation of emotional value she suggests to use *imagineering* as an approach. Holbrook (2001: 139) criticizes this concept as „a gloriously upbeat, positive and opportunistic picture of consumer culture full of millennial optimism". According to Prahalad and Ramaswamy (2004: 89) this concept is still company-centric, and treats customers as „human props in a carefully staged performance".

Morgan (2010) finds Ritzer et al.'s (1997) and Prahalad and Ramaswamy's (2004) criticism unfair to Pine and Gilmore (1999) who in fact stress that experiences are events that engage individuals in a personal way and that the most valued forms of experience do not just entertain but offer some kind of personal transformation (e.g. as health, wellness, spiritual or cultural skills). Lugosi (2007) emphasises that some memorable experiences happen spontaneously, therefore the question has to be asked as to whether memorable experiences should be managed at all. However, the staged performance, gustatory experience that Gillespie (2001) describes certainly suggests that some memorable experiences can, may even need to be managed and yet they will still remai authentic.

As Gibbs and Ritchie (2010) say, customers may require various experiences and differing levels of staff support and interaction across a range of situations. Gentile et al. (2007) posit that the best experiences are often co-created. For Graefe and Vaske (1987) the key characteristics of tourist experience are:

- emotional involvement of the tourist,

- significant interaction between tourists and tourism system,
- active participation in the experience.

To conclude, most of the literature shares a point of view according to what experience-centric management needs to move from a focus on staging performances to one on creating the space in which customers take an active part and co-create their own experiences.

4.2. Concept of experience co-creation

Prahalad and Ramaswamy (2000, 2002, 2004a, 2004b) a decade ago suggested that the locus of economic value creation was shifting from the firm's research and development department to the interaction between the firm and the consumer. They were one of the main co-creators of a research area commonly referred to as value co-creation. Value creation is a process describing the conversion of company resources into customer value (Chikán, 2003). The concepts of co-creation and value have assumed central importance in marketing theory. Co-creation refers to the processes by which both consumers and producers collaborate, or otherwise participate in value creation. Within this perspective, consumers are assumed to create value-in-use and co-create value with organizations, thus realizing their potential to utilize consumption to demonstrate knowledge, distinct and expertise; but also to construct, represent, and maintain their identity (Firat and Venkatesh, 1995); and form social networks (Holt, 1995).

Co-creation is neither new, nor specific to 21st century. Rather, by aknowledging that production and consumption are two sides of the same coin, co-creation is intrinsic to all forms of capitalist and non-capitalist economies. Nevertheless, recent social transformations such as the emergence of the internet, and in particular its user-generated version commonly called Web 2.0, have moved practices of co-creation to the center of a firm's economic value creation (Ritzer and Jurgenson, 2010).

4.2.1. The definitions of value

Value is one of the most controversial issues in the marketing literature (e.g. Sanchez-Fernandez and Iniesta-Bonillo, 2007). Value – complex and multidimensional – can be perceived to have different meanings depending on time, situation, or person

(Holbrook, 2006). Value can also be understood as a symbolic meaning (Shankar et al., 2009); as a value-added concept (Woodruff and Flint, 2006); as a linking value (Cova and Cova, 2002); as value-in-use (Vargo and Lusch, 2004), and as experience value (Holbrook and Hirschman, 1982, Holbrook, 1999). The perception of value can be explained through the idea of fragmentation, whereby contemporary consumers may customize value and meaning to achieve their life or career goals (Firat et al., 1995). For example one consumer may buy a Versace dress because it suits her whereas another consumer may be attracted to Versace's cultural value. Value represents not only the functional and economic value of goods and services, but also the consumer's interpretation of consumption objects, including products, brands, and services (Lawrence and Phillips, 2002).

Value co-creation has moved beyond the consumer's purchasing power and the functional purposes of products to focus on the symbolic meaning of consumption, thus companies need to understand how consumers value their set of life projects and how they enact their life narratives (Arnould and Price, 2000). Many marketing studies have revealed how collective consumers co-create the symbolic meaning of consumption (e.g. Amis and Silk, 2010; Cova and Pace, 2006; Leigh et al., 2006; Muniz and O'Guinn, 2001; Muniz and Schau, 2005). For example a recent study by Schau et al. (2009) explored collective value creation within several brand communities and provided a comprehensive review of brand value creation processes.

Gronroos's (2008) argues that while terms 'value creation' and 'create value' are frequently used in the literature, their meaning is a subject of various interpretations. Consequently, he focuses on value creation as the customer's creation of value-in-use. Value-in-use means that the customer as the user is partner in a business engagement that creates value. With that in mind, he considers that value creation is not an all-encompassing process – the design, development, and manufacturing of resources are not part of value creation, i.e. they just facilitate customers' value creation. The total process that leads to value-in-use for customers is needed to enable value creation, but all parts of it are not necessary part of value creation for the customer. Basically, production is generation of potential value, whereas usage is generation of real value.
He suggests that co-creation of value can take place only if interactions between the firm and the customer occur. If there are no direct interactions, no value co-creation is possible, while during interactions, the customer as co-producer can influence the firm's production process.
During direct interactions with customers, firms get opportunities to engage themselves with their customers' value creation and become co-creators of value as well. Outside direct interactions, customers' value creation with resources obtained from a supplier

or otherwise available is sole value creation. Outside direct interactions firms cannot be sole value creators, only value facilitators by developing, designing, manufacturing, and delivering resources required by customers.

The view of company and consumer as value co-creators has changed significantly in recent decades. Strategic attention has moved beyond the market orientation's emphasis on consumers over products (e.g. Jaworski and Kohli, 1993), to emphasize how consumers create symbolic meaning and value via consumption (e.g. Firat and Dholakia, 2006). Wikstrom (1996) suggests that marketing philosophy does not focus anymore on how companies create value for consumers, but rather on how they create value with consumers, signaling a change from a producer–consumer perspective to a co-creation perspective – as it is referred to within service-dominant logic of marketing (see Vargo and Lusch, 2008). In parallel, strategic brand communication has also shifted from telling stories to consumers, to sharing stories with consumers. A rich literature on value co-creation shows how interaction, dialogue, involvement, and consumption between companies and consumers play important roles in the co-creation of value (Etgar, 2008; Prahalad and Ramaswamy, 2004; Vargo and Lusch, 2004).

The concept of co-creation has emerged as one of the most important marketing paradigms. According to the concept of co-creation, consumers no longer occupy the end of the value chain; but, they assume central importance in the processes of value creation.
Based on Gabriel and Lang (2008) consumers have showed that despite of the best marketing efforts to control and manipulate them, they behavior is many times unpredictable and inconsistent. Increasing attention is being paid to how consumers can engage in the co-creation of value through individual co-creation experiences and interaction with brands, companies, and other consumers (Prahalad and Ramaswamy, 2004).

What the above literature review indicates that it is not only the role of the firm to change to become an experience enabler, and resource provider for value co-production, but it is the role of the consumer, too. Many terms have been used in an effort to capture the new consumer roles: prosumer, produser, protagonist, post-consumer, consum-actor, etc. (Cova és Dalli, 2009). This might be confusing, but what all these terms have in common is that they converge to describe more active and constructive consumers. A good opportunity to investigate this question is the recent rise of Web 2.0, the ground zero for making processes of production and consumption indistinguishable. To paraphrase Ritzer and Jurgenson (2010), Web 2.0 represents the new means of co-production.

Of course, more enabling and motivating factors contributes to the consumers' value co-creation – such as quest for authenticity and customization, new technology, community and social experience (Fischer and Smith, 2011), or information access, global perspective, quest for creative expression and activity (Prahalad and Ramaswamy, 2004), as Chapter 2 already discussed these topics earlier.

4.2.3. Service-dominant paradigm

Before introducing of Prahalad and Ramaswamy's value co-creation concept, first the analyses of the marketing theory is discussed, as a theoretical frame of the concept. The service-dominant logic as a marketing paradigm (Vargo and Lusch, 2004) contradicts traditional, product-dominant marketing paradigm, and calls for the complete reevaluation of marketing thinking. This new dominant logic focuses on services rather than on products, on intangible rather than on tangible goods, on relationship rather than on one-time transaction. Based on Vargo and Lusch (2004) reasons this with the recognition that truly important resources are not physical, operand resources, but so-called operant resources, such as knowledge and skills.

This paradigm forms a theoretical frame, which is able to encompass several alternative marketing perspectives, and creates a relevant soil for them – such as customer and market orientation, service marketing, relationship marketing, quality management, resource management, network analysis, and value co-creation. What is also common about these concepts, is that all of them view marketing as a social and economic process. The thesis or so-called foundational premises of the emerging new paradigm are (Vargo and Lusch, 2004):

1. the application of specialized skills and knowledge is the fundamental unit of exchange
2. indirect exchange masks the fundamental unit of exchange
3. goods are distribution mechanism for service provision
4. knowledge is the fundamental source of competitive advantage
5. all economies are services economies
6. the customer is always a co-producer
7. the enterprise can only make value propositions
8. a service-centered view is customer oriented and relational

According to Vargo and Lusch (2004) the service-dominant perspective should always carry the recognition that customization. The customer is part of the production, so customization should involve the customer. In this frame, tangible goods are viewed as mediators of services, the markets are perceived as streams of services, and not as place of product units' exchange.

Advertising, as one-side communication, is advised to be interchanged with two-sided, interactive dialogue. Dialogue should be continuous and personalized. The new marketing should be treated as a strategic field, and should help the planning and developing business processes between organization units of the firm.

Prahalad's (2004: 23) concern is that Vargo and Lusch „do not go far enough", because value co-creation should be experience-centric, and not service-dominant. The new perspective enables us to redefine concept such as brand (experiences defines a brand), the role of exchange on the market (market as forum), and innovation (innovation of experience environments). As next, these concepts get to the focus of analyses.

4.2.4. Definining value co-creation

Co-creation of experiences, as a theoretical construct, reflects the consumer as taking an active part in consuming and producing values, moreover, it deals with customer involvement in defining and designing the experience. The concept of value co-creation deals with the customers as serving themselves (Meuter et al., 2000), cooperating with the service providers (Vargo & Lusch, 2004), and adopting various roles in interaction with people and products (Vargo & Lush, 2008).

Prahalad (2004) discuss five modes how companies try to engage customers as co-producers into value creation process:

1. Firms try to persuade customers through advertising and promotions, these try to engage them emotionally, if not physically, in the act of coproduction.
2. The second phase of customer involvement is self-service (e.g. gas station, IKEA), which is a transfer of work from the firm to the customer. In this sense, the customer is a co-producer.
3. When a firm use the concept of staged experience, it constructs the context and the customer is a part of it (e.g. Disney world). The consumer is involved and engaged, but the context is firm driven.

4. In case a firm allows to a customer to navigate his/her way through the firm's system to solve a problem (e.g. call centers). This means a transfer of work, use of the customer's time and his/her skills.
5. In the fifth phase the consumers are getting involved in co-designing and coproducing products and services. Consumers have work, service and risk transferred from the firm, but they can also both benefit.

The common in the five perspectives is that although work and risk are shared, the firm decides how it will engage the customer the firm decides. Despite the fact they are recent solutions on the market, they do not take consumer trends into consideration yet. These major consumer trends are: the consumers are better and better informed and take part in various community networks, the convergention of (digital) technologies, global distribution of information.

Although in the focus of value co-creation is the experience and not the service, its general ideas are do not differ from those of service-dominant logic. The service-dominant logic's sixth foundational premise „the customer is always a coproducer" is even very similar to the main idea behind Prahalad and Ramaswamy's value co-creation concept. However, Prahalad (2004) in a reaction to Vargo and Lusch's work highlights that:

- customers are not isolated (customer communities are formed);
- the outcome of the engagements is the co-creation of value, and what is co-created is the experience; physical products and services are the artifacts around which personalized experiences are co-created;
- for this new building blocks are needed (e.g. dialogue);
- firms should cooperate and form networks, and they must work together to provide a unique co-creation experience.

4.2.5. The concept of value co-creation

Based on Prahalad and Ramaswamy (2004), the locus of value co-creation process of a business are the consumers and their co-creation experience. The consumer together with other customers and the firm jointly create the value, while the customer is taking an active role in value searching, producing and extracting. Based on their view, the firm's role is to engage the consumer in the definition and co-creation of a unique value, while firms applying a traditional marketing approach define and create the value for the customer in advance. The new, consumer- and experience-centric value co-creation concept views products and services as experience mediators.

Figure 7: The DART-model (elements of value co-creation)

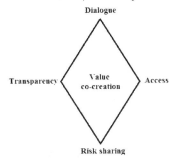

Source: adopted from Prahalad and Ramaswamy (2004)

Since the demand is various, the value creation process should enable a big variety of co-creation experiences. The context and the level of customer involvement and engagement contribute to the formation of personal meaning, and to the perceived uniqueness of the co-created experience. According to Prahalad and Ramaswamy (2004) the building blocks of value co-creation are **dialogue, access, transparency and risk sharing** – which form the so-called DART model (see Figure 7).

The concept promises new capabilities for firms and service providers. The management will not be responsible anymore for the quality of products, services and processes, but for the quality of the experience from value co-creation process. This quality depends on how wide is the infrastructure which enables interaction between the firm and the consumer. The firm needs to effectively innovate its experience environment, which facilitates a diversity of co-created experiences. Products and services are considered to be parts of the experience environment, where individual consumers create and personalize their experiences.

Table 2: Traditional and experience-based innovation

	Traditional innovation	Experience-based innovation
Aim of innovation	products and processes	experience environment
Basis of experience	product and service offers	experience of co-creation
Value creation perspective	firm create the value	the value is co-created
Focus of development	cost, quality, speed, modularity	granularity, extensibility, connectivity, upgradeability

The view of technology	features and functions, technology and system integration	facilitator of the experience, experience integration
The focus of infrastructure	supporting the products and services	supporting the co-creation of personalized experiences

Source: Prahalad and Ramaswamy (2004a: 71)

Based on the concept formulation of a flexible experience network has a crucial importance for firms. This experience network facilitates the customization of experiences for customers. The role of the firm and the consumer interweave, which results a unique value co-creation, a personal experience (Prahalad and Ramaswamy, 2004).

Table 3: Comparing traditional and experience customization

	Traditional customization	Experience customization
Customization perspective	the segment of one	the experience of one
Focus of customization	the one products and services	customization of interactions with experience environment
Mode of customization	menu of fixtures, features, costs and speed	events, the context of events, personal involvement, personal meaning
View of value chain	realization of customized product and service variety formed by modularity	facilitation of variety of customized experiences through heterogeneous interactions

Source: Prahalad and Ramaswamy (2004a: 88)

The authors clarify what cannot be seen as a concept of co-creation: the transfer nor outsourcing of activities to customers nor a marginal customization of products and services; nor is a scripting or staging of customer events around the firm's various offerings. It is stated that these kinds of solutions no longer satisfy most customers today. What Prahalad and Ramaswamy (2004) describe as co-creation concept is much more fundamental: **it involves value co-creation through personalized interactions that are to a specific consumer.**

In case of any person, value co-creation (and not the offering) means the basis of the unique value. The co-creation experience depends highly on individuals, thus a firm cannot create anything of value without the engagement of individuals. The market will be increasingly more like a forum organized around value co-creation.

Table 4: The comparison of traditional perspective and co-creation concept

	Traditional view			Value co-creation concept		
Premise	Firm creates the value	Products and services are the basis of value	Customers forms the demand towards the firm's offers	The customer and the firm are the co-producers of value	The co-creation experience is the basis of value	The person is in the locus of value co-creation
Implication	The interface between the firm and the consumer is locus of value extraction	Creation of multiply offers	Customization of offers and staging of experiences	Customer – firm interaction is locus of value co-creation	Variety of co-creation experiences through heterogeneous interactions	Personalization of the co-creation experience
Manifestation	Focus on value chains and the quality of company processes	Focus on innovation of technology and product	Focus on management of supply chain and demand	Focus on the quality of customer – firm interactions	Focus on innovating experience environments	Focus on experience networks

Source: Prahalad and Ramaswamy (2004a)

But the element of collaboration, while important, is not the central point made by Prahalad and Ramaswamy. Rather, what they saw as the role of production and consumption was that such a mode of co-creation guarantees the delivery of 'unique' value to consumers (Foster, 2011). Co-creation, in other words, ensures that the experience of consuming a product or service must vary from one consumer to another because it is, by definition, non-standardized. Thus, Prahalad and Ramaswamy make the case that any company that internalizes the idea of co-creation and puts it into practice will be rewarded by defending its offerings against commoditization, while at the same time benefiting from an ability to charge premium prices for the co-created product and service.

Payne et al. (2008) investigated experience co-creation as a value creating process. Their research was realized during three workshops held for leaders and managers, and it analyzed the value co-creation process between customers and the company, while their conceptualized value co-creation based on Vargo and Lusch (2004).

They formed a process-based value co-creation framework consisting of three main components:
- (1) customer value-creating processes (which describes the processes, resources and practices which customers use to manage their activities),

- (2) the supplier value-creating processes (it includes the processes, resources and practices which the supplier uses to manage its business and its relationships with customer and other relevant stakeholders),
- (3) the encounter processes (the processes and practices of interaction and exchange that take place within customer and supplier relationships).

Figure 8: The conceptual framework for value creation

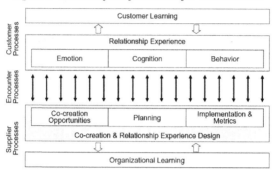

Source: Payne et al. (2008: 86)

The authors highlight that customer experience and value creation is being defined by encounter processes rather than by the product itself. According to them, the value creation process with the customer would be viewed as a dynamic, interactive, nonlinear, and often unconscious process.

Investigation of experience co-creation faces an increasing research interest lately, however theoretical conceptualization and empirical result is still in a developing phase (Payne et al., 2008).

4.2.6. Experience co-creation concept in tourism

Binkhorst and Dekker, advocates of experience co-creation concept in tourism, pointed out in their 2009 paper that **experience co-creation leads to increased value both for tourists and the tourism sector in the destination.** The concept of creativity is used by several authors to explain why consumption is increasingly driven by the need for self-development (Florida, 2002; Richards & Wilson, 2006). It is argued that the solution for creativity, innovation and involvement can be found in the concept of co-creation, because co-creation increases value for human beings in the experience economy. (Binkhorst and Dekker 2009).

Prebensen and Foss (2011) investigates tourist experience co-creation from consumer perspective. In their research they ask, **how the consumer create added value regarding an experience derived from a tourism service.** The research results show that interaction, participation and involvement in various activities all create more positive customer feelings in various settings and situations (host–guest, guest–guest and guest–family), and thus enhance the value for the participants. The findings that the level of consumer participation in a certain activity impacts satisfaction, is also supported by other studies (e.g. Ryan, 2002).

Only few academic authors have taken up research into the managerial as opposed to the behavioral, sociological and psychological aspects of the consumer experience paradigm (Morgan, 2010). This was initially true in tourism, where destination management appeared slow to accept the implications of this perspective (see King, 2002 and Williams, 2006). Payne et al. (2008) identify that except of Prahalad and Ramaswamy's DART model (see Figure 7) (and the model formed by them – see Figure 8) there is no other theoretical frame or model, which would help the business sector to apply the co-creation concept.

To bridge the gap between the new tourist and the more traditional marketing oriented DMO, the new marketing thoughts should provide a different conceptualization of the whole tourism consumption experience (Li and Petrick, 2007). According to Li and Petrick co-creation between tourists and providers should be the answer. Co-creation **involves tourists' active involvement and interaction with the supplier in every aspect, from product design to product consumption** (Payne et al., 2008).

According to O'Dell (2005) sites of market production, the spaces in which experiences are staged and consumed can be likened to stylized landscapes that are strategically planned, laid out and designed, but also have an impact on consumer's imagination are so called **experiencescapes.** These experiencescapes are landscapes of experience that are not only organized by producers (from place marketers and city planners to local private enterprises), but are also actively sought after by consumers. They are places of enjoyment, pleasure, and entertainment, as well as the meeting grounds of diverse groups. Such an experiencescapes is for example Stockholm's Skanzen, Budapest's Zoo, or Hard Rock Café anywhere in the world.

However, O'Dell is arguing, that experiencescapes involve more than culturally organized powers of the imagination or globally shared recipes for the packaging of fun; they also include a spatial component that should be understood. The commodification of and search for experiences has a material base that is itself anchored in space. They occur in specific places, such as stores, museums, cities, sporting arenas, shopping centers, neighborhood parks and well-known tourist attractions. The conceptualization of experiencescape seems to be similar to Prahalad and Ramaswamy's experience environment, however its definition takes rather a sociological and cultural perspective, than business view, and it does not take into account the concept of experience co-creation.

Increasing number of tourism service providers apply business strategies of co-creation. *Budapest Underguide* offers customized, experience-centric tours to its customers, and promise them to travel to Budapest as they are visiting a friend. Also Budapest-based *Program Deluxe* offers interactive programs to small groups and individual travelers, such as a cooking class with a pro chef, or personal meeting with an artist in her/his home. The *I feel London* webpage (www.ifeellondon.com) based on the one's actual mood (romantic, energetic, hangover etc.) suggests sights, restaurants, bars and other attractions to the user. The *Dine with the Dutch* service provider organizes dinners to the homes of local families, to make the tourist experience very authentic. Most of the recent city guides are in a form of mobile application, and offer an interactive and customized interface.

4.3. Experience-centric perspective in tourism destinations

The destination management has also started to apply the experience-centric approach. The concept of experience was not unfamiliar for destinations, however, it was first considered to be rather a matter of context than a matter of content; they believed it to be a natural supplementary product, not an innovation that could be formed and improved (Stamboulis and Skayannis, 2003). Part of the destination management organizations appeared slow to accept the implications of this perspective. King (2000) criticized them for being too focused on promoting the physical attributes of the destination, despite travel being increasingly more about experiences, fulfillment and rejuvenation. Williams (2006) called for a change of perspective which **focused less on destinations and more on the consumers themselves.** In his view point, tourism and hospitality failed to take up the fundamental challenge to the orientation of marketing that the experience concept offers. Tourism experience management concept is emphasizing the centrality of the tourist and its consumer experience.

The motivation for visiting a destination usually does not derive from its physical qualities but from a strong spiritual and emotional image, the destination

experience assumed by the tourist. For example, when tourists in Verona visit Juliet's balcony, they indulge in a romantic fantasy about Shakespeare's drama. This overwhelming experience serves as the main motivation for the visit that is the base of the destination product. According to Richards (2001) it can easily be proved that some tourist destinations are positioned as experiences – e.g. Austria, Iceland, or India.

The demand side has changed, too. Today's consumers have quite different attitude towards consumption than previous generations. Tourists are looking for unique activities, tailored experiences, special interest focus, experiences in a lifestyle destination setting, living culture, creative spaces and creative spectacles (Gross & Brown, 2006). Tourists and consumers in general are not only better educated and wealthier, but also have access to more information than ever before.

Experiences tend to determine the value of destinations and DMOs are increasingly using this in positioning their destinations on the market (e.g.: *Incredible India* marketing campaign). "The demand is growing for travel that engages the senses, stimulates the mind, includes unique activities, and connects in personal ways with travelers on an emotional, psychological, spiritual or intellectual level" (Arsenault and Gale, 2004 in Canadian Tourism Commission Research Report 7: 21).

A Canadian research shows (Arsenault and Gale, 2004) that learning experiences (e.g. photography workshops, wine tasting), and tourism products which enable contacts with the local community (such as cooking, visiting farms, and being welcomed into the homes of locals), are growing in popularity. This also holds true for all sorts of experimental, practical and interactive activities. Tourists want to take a peek behind the scenes. Furthermore, the social dynamics connected with travel, getting to know new people, reinforcing old friendships and making new ones, spending time with relatives, and sharing of experiences, are also considered to be more and more important.

Recent tourism marketing research increasingly focuses on the experience of tourists and the cultural context of a destination. Lichrou et al. (2008) assert that a destination must not only be regarded as a physical space. Places have intangible, cultural historical and dynamic aspects too (Lichrou et al., 2008). They believe that it is not about the product as a result, but about understanding the intangible, a process of experience, the dreams and fantasies of consumers, the meeting of people, interaction between hosts and visitors and other tourists. It concerns a dynamic context in which destinations are simultaneously consumed and produced. Based on the fact that tourists have an image of a tourism destination even though they have never been there, the authors suggest to consider **destinations metaphorically, as narratives rather than**

products. This view leaves a room for the concept of interaction, co-creation, and for the notion of the tourist as participant instead of spectator.

The role of experience starts to obtain key importance concerning destination positioning and marketing. King (2002) draws attention to the fact that DMOs need to have a complete turn in their attitudes; they should no longer identify themselves as the promotional agents of destinations. In addition, the author states that they should concentrate on creating and communicating such travel experiences, which combine the destination's important values as a brand and its resources (environmental, cultural, gastronomical etc.) with the aims of travelers and the needs of consumers.

The strategy of experience management can also be observed concerning investments and marketing processes. Stamboulis and Skayannis (2003) consider creating myths essential for the existence of experiences; the narrative overwriting the text written by signs. That is a process rich in knowledge, which cannot possibly occur if the tourism service provider, for example a DMO, focuses only on services. Even during the phase of production (including the creation of experience schemes and the application of certain methods and techniques) the previously obtained knowledge – concerning the possible main interests of the consumers (Stamboulis and Sayannis, 2003) and the future experiences assumed by the consumers (Ooi 2005, Writz et al., 2003) – has to be put to use. Competencies concerning information and service provision, the intelligence of the company plays a key role, and the interaction with the consumer has to have a more active role as well. Therefore business innovations have to be centered on creating new experience-schemes. To achieve that interactive learning processes are needed; moreover, the strategy of experience-based tourism has to rely rather on the incomprehensible, ideal resources, than on material resources (for example environment and infrastructure).

Tourism mediators play a crucial role in creating tourist experiences during destination visiting, because they direct the tourists' attention. Ooi (2005) defines these tourism mediators as service providers, individuals or goods, which give advice to tourists what to notice, how to consume various tourism products. Tour operators, tour and program providers, tourism promotional authorities, tour guides, travel reviews, guidebooks, and friendly locals all belong to this category.

Despite the fact that various concepts and perceptions exist about tourist experience, they all agree that the appearance of an experience is characterized with a dynamic process. Tourists have different experiences, and they pay attention to different things, even if they all participate the same activity at the same time and place. The mediators help to direct their attention and gazes, and also form the tourists' interpretations of tourism sights and sites. Tourists often visit a place for a relatively short period of time, they lack local knowledge, so to consume more and better from the visited destination, they are seeking a shortcut to experience the place, and this shortcut is offered by tourism mediators. However tourists construct their experiences based on their own (social, cultural etc.) background and interest, according to Ooi (2005) tourist mediators contribute to this process. They heighten or hinder the tourist's experience-involvement.

The consumer experience involvement plays an important role in experience creation, moreover it is one of its main conditions (see e.g. Mossberg, 2007, O'Sullivan and Spangler, 1998, Pine and Gilmore, 1999, Prahalad and Ramaswamy, 2004). Most of the researchers agree that involvement happens at four levels: (1) physical / sensorial, (2) mental, (3) emotional, (4) social level.

The experience co-creation is a process directed by the consumer, which can start anytime when s/he is emotionally, mentally and physically available, and if s/he can control the situation, in which the experience is formed (Prebensen and Foss, 2011).

Based on the experience continuum model (see Figure 4), the guided tours can influence the consumer's experience involvement in the following ways.

In case of a staged experience, if the tourist has a chance of free choice of what to focus on, how much time should s/he spend with a given activity (etc.), s/he will be able of engagement and formation of experience, therefore the possibility to create a memorable experience with personal meaning is bigger. The service provider applying staged experience concept aims to stage and perform the experience on high quality level, and that is how it tries to engage the customer to the experience, however, this does not necessary provide a high degree of freedom for the customer, because it does not allow customization.

If a tour provider is applying traditional product oriented approach, and not experience-centric approach, it might happen that the tourist faces limitations during experience-involvement (e.g. not enough time available for a sight), so the experience consumption does not fulfill, and the experience might not become meaningful and memorable, or the other extreme prevails and the experience will become memorable in negative quality. Mainly the needs of passive tourists with 'attraction check-list' mentality is possible to compensate with this type of service, while others can feel themselves limited or might find the tour boring.

Tour providers using methods of experience co-creation approach aims to engage the customer by offering big number of interaction points, and forms possibilities for experience co-creation and customization. By enabling customization it creates optimal degree of freedom for the tourist's experience involvement. Meanwhile the consumer can decide to what extent and how s/he wishes to be involved to the experience creation. This requires a higher degree activity and participation from the tourist.

4.4. The conceptual frame of experience-centric management

Based on available literature sources the Conceptual Frame of Experience-centric Management was created. The Conceptual Frame (Table 5) is a synthesis which also serves as an analytical frame during the research process.

Table 5: The Conceptual Frame of Experience-centric Management

Conceptual framework of staged experience:
<ul><li>Staged experience is the source of added value.</li><li>Drama should be the focal metaphor of business. Company is viewed as a „theatre", workers are „actors", customers are an „audience" or „guests", physical environment is a „stage", and „show" is performed by experience (service) providers.</li><li>Finding the value of an experience for a customer is significant, and it also forms an essential element of a competitive brand.</li><li>Drama marks the interaction between a company and the customer. The engagement of the customer and the importance of the experience depend on the level and quality of interaction. Consequently, deeper level of customer involvement is the company's priority.</li><li>Optimal experience environment and its props enable higher level of interaction and deeper involvement into the experience.</li><li>Sustainable competitiveness can only be reached by creating unique and memorable experiences. The most valuable form of experience does not only entertain, but insures the possibility of personal development.</li><li>The company standardizes the creation of experience, so heterogeneity of the service is reduced.</li><li>Frontline workers should build their personality traits into their roles.</li><li>Scripts should be written in case of each interaction situation, and for all stages.</li><li>Metaphors of drama and storytelling should be applied.</li></ul>
Conceptual framework of co-creation experience concept:
<ul><li>The individual and his/her experience co-creation are in the center of the value creation process. The consumer and the company co-create the value, so experience co-creation is the basis of value.</li><li>Consumer co-creates the experience with the organization and other consumers, while she is an active participant in value searching, producing and abstraction.</li><li>Consumers do not stand alone, they form a consumer community.</li><li>Involvement of consumer into experience co-creation and unique value creation is at the organization's best interest.</li></ul>

• To enhance experience co-creation with the consumer, organizations should cooperate and form a network.
• Interaction between the consumers and the organization is the locus of value co-creation.
• Creating an experience environment in which consumers can have active dialogues and co-construct personalized experiences; product may be the same but customers can construct different experiences. The organization should allow an experience variety for the consumer.
• The organization should effectively innovate its experience environment to allow variety of experience creation.
• The context and the level of consumer involvement contribute to personal meaning formulation and the perceived uniqueness of experience co-creation.
• The essential building blocks of experience co-creation are dialogue, access, transparency and risk-benefits.
• Products and services are parts of experience environment, where individual consumers participate in experience co-creation.
• Products and services are only intermediaries of (co-created) experiences.
Conceptual framework of experience-centric management perspective:
• It is a management of experiences, and not products.
• Treats experience as content, formable and developable, and not only as a part of a product, nor simply as a context.
• Believes that on the consumer side, travelling is increasingly about experiences, fulfillment and rejuvenation.
• Enhancing active participation and involvement of the consumer.
• Assigns a high importance to interaction with the consumer.
• It results in a knowledge-intensive process, which is not possible if the organization's main focus is on service provision.
• Consumers' anticipated experiences and points of interest are investigated.
• These anticipated experiences and points of interest are utilized in product, method and experience environment development.
• New experience themes are in the center of innovation.
• Its strategy builds on intangible resources and utilization of goodwill, rather than on material resources.
• Experience-centric perspective demonstrates itself through investments and marketing activity, too.
• Believes that the creation of myths and stories ensures a steady foundation for successful experiences. Narrative should overcome facts and script.
• On destination level, encourages active participation of local community in creating tourism experience.

Source: own compilation (2013)

Chapter 2, 3, 4 as literature review parts, define the main and relating concepts, investigate the theoretical contributions and existing research results, and end with formation of a conceptual frame. All this represents a relevant starting point and background for the start of empirical research.

5. INTRODUCTION TO RESEARCH METHODOLOGY

5.1. The aim and subject of the research

The main goal of the research was to explore the means of experience-creation realized through the interaction between provider and consumer, thus the research examines the experience-creation of the consumer from the viewpoint of the provider.

I have also aimed to collect and process the experiences and know-how of tourism service providers putting the experience-centric approach, more precisely the staged experience concept and the experience co-creation concept into practice, while also examining the effects of latter concepts on the consumer experience.

The central research question was formulated as follows:

- *How can destination experience mediators influence the experience creation of a tourist?*

The subjects of the research are destination experience mediators – program agencies and tour companies – offering city sightseeing tours for visitors. The service providers are destination experience mediators as their activity focuses on the interpretation of the tourist attractions and the local culture of the destination. I chose Budapest as the location of my research.

5.2. Research questions and hypotheses

The research was realized with the aid of the following research questions and their corresponding assumptions and hypotheses:

Question 1: How and to what extent does the experience-centric approach, more precisely the staged experience concept and the experience co-creation concept determine the management approach and activity of destination experience mediators?

The 'how' interrogative refers to the mode of manifestation of the experience-centric approach, respectively the above mentioned two experience concepts, in the management and marketing activity of the service providers.

The research question of exploratory profile is about to be answered through the analysis of collected data based on the Conceptual Frame (Table 5).

In relation to the first research question, the following assumptions were made:

- **Assumption 1:** The experience-centric approach is mostly characteristic of small-scale tour providers.
- **Assumption 2:** In the case of alternative tour providers, the experience co-creation concept is the ruling principle.
- **Assumption 3:** The staged experience concept is not predominant among any of the tour providers.

For answering the research question no. 1, two qualitative research methods were realized: interview and observation. Interviewees were managers and tour guides (i.e. who directly interact with the consumers). Observations cover the tours themselves, where and when the consumption of the provided service and experience happens.

Question 2: How tour providers influence the consumer experience created during the tour?

Following the aim of the thesis, the consumer experience is being investigated from the perspective of the provider's experience creation activity. Thus on consumer's side the research covers solely those factors influenced by the provider, while the emphasis is on experience creation analysis. The sub-questions are the followings:

1. How consumers evaluate the interaction with the tour provider?
2. How consumers evaluate the experience environment formed by the tour provider?
3. To what extent do the consumers perceive the tour to be customized?
4. How consumers evaluate their own experience-involvement? Does the provider support the experience creation process?
5. To what extent do the consumers find the tour experience memorable and authentic?
6. How are these influencing factors and experience outcomes (such as memorability and authenticity) related to each other?

Figure 9: The structural model of hypotheses

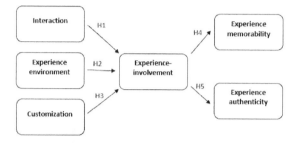

Source: own compilation (2013)

In relation to the second research question, the following assumptions were determined:

- H1: Interaction contributes to the degree of the consumer's involvement into a given experience.
- H2: The experience environment contributes to the involvement into a given experience.
- H3: Perceived customization contributes to the involvement into a given experience.
- H4: Involvement into a given experience affects the memorability of that experience.
- H5: Involvement into a given experience affects the authenticity of that experience.

Comparing the results of the two research questions, the following hypotheses are examined:

- H6: Tour providers preferring the experience-centric approach are able to reach a higher degree of experience-involvement regarding the role of the tourist in experience-creation than providers preferring the non-experience-centric approach.
- H7: Tour providers mainly preferring the experience co-creation concept have the most success in involving the tourist into the process of experience-creation.

To find an answer for the central research question, primary data collection was carried out with the triangulation-method, had three main sources (company leadership, employees directly interacting with consumers, and the consumers themselves), put three research methods into practice (interview with the management, observation, questionnaire), and consisted of three separate sections (interview with the management, interview with the tour guide, observation and questionnaire during the course of the tour). These formerly mentioned factors allow a deeper exploration of the research problem and contribute to the reliability and validity of the research results.

Figure 10: Data collection sources

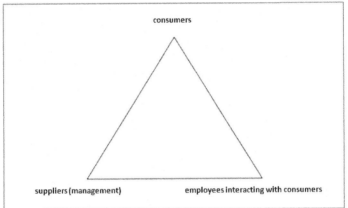

Source: own compilation (2013)

The three data collecting methods (interview, observation, and questionnaire) aimed to investigate the experience creation between provider and tourist by mutually compensating their disadvantages with their advantages. The reason for choosing such a complex methodology was – according to the aim of the research – to get a deeper and more comprehensive exploration of the various methods of tourism experience creation (from a business point of view) between provider and tourist, within the boundaries of the available research resources. The lack of research resources (personal, financial, temporal) tend to somewhat limit the potential of a given research. Consequently, with the support of my supervisor, I chose a research methodology which meets several requirements:

- capable of collecting an ideal amount and quality of complex data,
- combining various methods increases the reliability and validity of the research,
- cost-effective,
- meets the requirements of a PhD thesis.

The connections between the research questions and the chosen methodology are demonstrated below in Table 6

Table 6: Research questions and methodology

Research questions	Subjects of the research	Methodology
(1) How is the experience-centric concept, more precisely the staged experience concept and the experience co-creation concept reflected in the management approach and operations of destination experience mediators?	tour providers – managers, tour guides, and the consumers themselves	qualitative: interviews and observation
(2) How does the tour provider influence the consumer experience-creation during the tour?	consumers	quantitative: questionnaire

Source: own compilation (2013)

Qualitative methodology was used to answer the first question of the research.

How and to what extent does the experience-centric approach, more precisely the staged experience concept and the experience co-creation concept determine the management approach and operations of tour providers?

Research methodology proposes to use flexible and unstructured techniques of qualitative research in case of explorative study (see Babbie, 2001, Malhotra and Simon, 2009, Ghauri and Gronhaug, 2011). The qualitative research helps to identify thinking patterns and opinions, and the deeper explanation of the researched problem (Sajtos and Mitev, 2007).
Qualitative in-depth interview was chosen as the most appropriate research technique to answer the question. During the interview I asked the company's management and the front line employees with the aim to collect primary data. Furthermore, observation technique was used to examine the manifestation of aspects and methods used during the service provision and the process of experience creation.

In-depth interview is a technique of exploratory methodology, while observation as a descriptive technique, complete the results from the exploratory phase. According to Sajtos and Mitev (2007) the results of an exploratory research provide a good basis for further casual research. Casual research (which appears in the second research question) should be applied, if the researcher knows the nature and structure of the problem, and the goal of the descriptive research to report about a given situation (Ghauri and Gronhaug, 2011).

6.1. Sampling and the characteristics of the sample

The **process of the sampling** in case of the first research question was defined accordingly (Churchill, 1995):

- *defining the target population:* (discrete target population) the tourism experience mediators – tour providers in 2012-2013.
- *identifying the sampling frame:* (a list compiled with the elements of the target population, which helps to select the units of the sampling) The sampling frame was created by listing and typology of all tour organizers of Budapest.

- *selecting a sampling procedure:* sampling by a random method: stratified sampling followed by systematic sampling.
- *determining the sample size:* (which is influenced by: how heterogeneous is the examined population, what is the budget, what is the purpose of the research, how much accuracy is needed) One manager interview per company
- *selecting the sample elements:* tour provider types (small-group, big-group, alternative)
  - *observation unit:* individual – manager

The **stratified sampling** is a random sampling method. The target population is divided into homogeneous and separable groups by a certain criteria. As next, sample units will be chosen from every group by a random method (e.g. simple random sampling, systematic sampling). The stratified sampling can be divided into two sub-groups: proportionally stratified and disproportionally stratified sampling.

The **systematic sampling** is a random sampling method. Its essence is that a starting point in the sampling frame is chosen randomly (for example the second company) and after that every „i-th" (for example fifth) element will be chosen.

During the sampling representativity was an aim, although the main goal of the research was not to reach representativity form the perspective of the location (Budapest). The main goal was to explore management approaches, methods and processes of certain tour types, to point out similarities, differences, and especially study their impact on customer experience. That was the reason why the sampling procedure did not prioritize the market share of certain tour types (certain tour types are more popular). The aspect was the equal representation of the examined tour types in the sample.

The sampling frame was evolved on the basis of the following tour types:
- **Small-group tour provider: 4 businesses**
- **Big-group tour provider: 3 businesses**
- **Alternative tour provider: 4 businesses**

The sampling frame of the research plan submitted in the dissertation proposal in 2012 differs from this final form. Originally it was planned to examine more tour types, but 'incentive' and 'organized group' tour types had to be eliminated from the sample, because of difficulties which aroused during data collection (see Limitations in Chapter 11). Finally, the sampling frame stayed focused on tours addressing only **leisure-type individual tourist**.

Small-group tour providers specialize on smaller size group tours, they usually organize walking tours, cycling tours and tours on segways for the tourists visiting Budapest. Some tours are guaranteed (it is realized even with 2 participants), but others are held only if a minimal number of participants is reached. Participants of the tours are individuals forming random groups, but pre-arranged small-group tours are also common. Small-group tour providers of the sample are **Budabike (BB)[3], Discover Budapest (DIS), Free Budapest Tours (FRE). Cityrama (CI)** is a provider of a small-group tours primary, but most of the tours are organized by bus, so they also share similarities with the second group of the sample (big group tours).

Big-group tours are mostly bus tours. These tours, serving the needs of leisure and individual tourists, are mostly guaranteed tours, while the group is formed randomly in most of the times. The sample of big-group tours includes: **RiverRide (RR),** a tour provider offering special, a 'floating bus' bus-boat tours; **Program Centrum (PC)** and **Eurama (EU)** provide hop-on hop-off type (HoHo) sightseeing tours.

Alternative tour providers typically organize special themed tours for which a particular type of demand has formed, and it became popular among Budapestians. From psychological perspective all the experiences gained in unusual environment, meaning a novelty for the individual, can be considered as tourist experience. Local sightseeing tours provide novelty for the participants from two reasons - they are guided in less well-known parts of the city, and they uncover rare information and hidden stories. These tours fill meanings into locations and spaces which were insignificant to the individual till then. The alternative tour providers are 'alternative', because they apply different methods and tools than the traditional tour providers. **Imagine Budapest (IG), Unique Hungary (UQ), BUPAP (BU),** and **Hosszulepes (HL)** participated in the research, as alternative tour providers.

The first research question is both exploratory and descriptive in nature – two research methods were used: qualitative interview and observation. Interviews were realized with the management and the tour guides. Observation technique was used to examine the interaction between the provider and the consumer, and to observe the experience environment on the spot of the tour.

One managerial and two tour guide interviews were performed with every tour provider of the sample. Additionally, at least two tours were observed per tour provider. In case

---

[3] the brackets show the abridgements of tour providers' names (used also in Chapter 8)

of observation the observed unit was the tour operator, the tourist or the group of participants.

The in-depth interview is an unstructured, direct, personal interview, in which a qualified interviewer realize a conversation with a respondent, with the aim of exploring his/her motivations, opinions, attitudes and feelings regarding a certain topic (Malhotra and Simon, 2009).

In-depth interviews are typically exploratory in nature that is why this technique was chosen to examine how the experience-centric approaches manifest themselves in the marketing and management activity of the tour providers. The in-depth interview was realized with the management and tour guides of the company (service provider).

Kvale (1996) distinguishes seven steps of the interview process:

1. Thematization: to clarify the goals of the interview and the concepts to explore
2. Planning: to plan the process that leads to an achievement of the research aim, and thinking over the ethical dimensions.
3. Realization of the interview
4. Writing: making a written copy or an extract from the interview
5. Analysis: to analyze the meaning of the collected data
6. Verification: checking the reliability and validity of the data and results
7. Reporting: communicate the result to others

According to Malhotra and Simon (2009) it is really important to ask questions during the interview, with the purpose to provoke valuable answers and to explore hidden thoughts.

Babbie (2001) suggests the followings:

- Questions are defined in less structured form than in case of questionnaires. The interview is a directed conversation, rather than a collection of certain information.
- For realization of a good interview active attention skills and conversation guidance skills are needed.
- The qualitative interview is iterative, flexible and constant, and not predetermined (Rubin and Rubin, 1995).
- During the interview the researcher should behave „socially fairly incompetent",

s/he should behave like does not understand the situation, and needs clarification and help even to understand basic things - the researcher is unconscious, who needs to be taught (Lofland and Lofland, 1995).

- The thread of the interviewee should not be interrupted,
- If the number of interview topics can be limited, it becomes easier to maintain the conversation flow while changing the topics, while one should be aware of the transition to keep it simple and logical (Rubin and Rubin, 1995).

In Malhotra and Simon's view (2009) characteristics of the in-depth interview (compared to other techniques) are: its structural complexity is at medium level, the in-depth analyzes of one responder is high, the disfigurations caused by of the questioner is quite high, the disfigurations because of interpretation is medium, the exploration and collection of unconscious information is between medium and high level, the exploration of innovative and sensitive information is of medium level, while the general utility of the interview technique is good.

According to Babbie (2001) the *strengths and weaknesses* of the in-depth interview are the followings:

- The main strength of the interview is the possibility of deep understanding, it is also flexible and usually cheap.
- A weakness of the interview is that it is not suitable for statistical analyzes of bigger populations.
- If we compare it with the questionnaire analysis, the validity of the results are typicaly higher, but the reliability is smaller.

6.3. The process of data collection – in-depth interviews

The qualitative in-depth interviews were carried out with a semi-structured method. The in-depth interview with the management took 60-100 minutes, while interviews with the tour guides took 15-35 minutes. Questioned raised to the management were formed based on the conceptual frame (Table 5), while the sequence of the questions were influenced by factors such as the interviewee's answers, the discussed topics and the progress of the conversation.

6.3.1. Data fixation

The interviews' sound was recorded. At the beginning of the interview the interviewees were informed about the research and its goals, and the recordings were made with their permissions. Besides notes were taken by the researcher (the author). Most of the interviews were made in headquarter of the tour providers, which enabled the researcher to get an insight into the organization's circumstances and atmosphere. After the realization of the interviews, extract-like transcripts were prepared by listening to the interviews repeatedly - nearly 60 pages of transcripts were made from the interviews with the managers.

6.3.2. The method of data analysis

After preparing the transcripts, key concepts and codes were defined following to the sub-questions' themes – with MS Excel program. While making the transcript (listening to the recordings repeatedly), the key words were determined. The sub-questions and key words (existing codes) were completed with information derived from the qualitative data (open codes).

The collected data (from interviews and observations) was analyzed by qualitative methods aiming to explore and describe. The descriptive profile is ensured by the conceptual frame. The exploratory profile made possible to explore the used strategies and methods through semi-structured interviews and „how" type questions, meanwhile taking attention to avoid influencing the interviewee with theoretical concepts. Although a part of the interview asked about theoretical concepts, this was performed only in the second part of the interview, after the exploratory section. So, while the descriptive research is built on data from the whole length of the interview, only the first part of the interview contributed to the exploratory part of the research.

As a result of the exploratory research, statements and assumptions, observed processes and situations were collected, which represent the tour provider's experiential knowledge and its manifestation. Although the process of triangulation raises the reliability and validity of the conclusions, the results are not generalizable because of the small sample size, however it serves as a good starting point for future research. In case of a descriptive research the sample size (11 providers) does not justify the statistical analysis, because the number of examined variables exceed the number of respondents. Although the qualitative methodology does not require multivariate data analysis or the representativeness of the results, the results should be comparable (requires to determine score-based values) in order to answer the assumptions.

6.3.3. The researcher's role

During the organization process of the interviews (through email and telephone) information about the research questions and goals were provided. The locations of the interviews were chosen by the interviewees, with the intention to increase their comfort. Most of the managerial interviews were realized in the tour provider's office. Most of the interviews took 80-90 minutes. Majority of the interviewees opened up during the first few questions, thanks to the short informal conversations in the beginning. Many of them indicated that they welcome the research, and they were pleased to talk about their views, work processes and methods. After or during the interviews some of them pointed out that the asked questions represent the theoretical formulation of practices which they were implementing often without knowing the concept. Questions about to the experience concept were asked at the end of the interviews. Before starting the interview they were informed only about the main questions of the research. The tour guide interviews were usually realized right after the tour. I asked them questions about their concepts and work methods: *What makes a tour to be excellent and memorable? What makes a good tour guide? What kind of methods do they use during the guiding? What kind of tour experience do they try to create?* The guides were also glad to take part in the research.

6.4. Methodology of observation

Observation belongs to the category of descriptive research. Its goal is to capture the behavior of people, the objects and events with the aim to collect information in a systematic way (Malhotra and Simon, 2009). During the process of observation the observer does not ask questions, and typically does not communicate with the observed people. The observation methods can be structured or unstructured, direct or indirect.

According to Malhotra and Simon (2009) in case of a structured observation the researcher defines the object and method of the observation in a detailed form, which reduces disfiguration and increases the reliability of the data. This technique can be applied if the problem is clearly defined and the sought information is specified.
In the present study:

- **The object of the observation:** interaction between the guide and the tourist, experience-involvement, customization and the experience environment.
- **The method of the observation:** the observer participates both in a hidden or unhidden form. The guide knows, but the tourists do not know that the researcher is present.

- **Definition of the problem:** How experience creation methods of the providers and guides manifest themselves in practice (during the tour)? How do the consumers react?

The **strengths and weaknesses** of the observation method (Malhotra and Simon, 2009):
- They enable to measure the real and not only the intended or preferred behavior.
- There is no interpretational disfiguration, and the disfigurations characteristic to the procedure of interviews can be avoided. However, this method is suitable only for collection of certain kinds of data, for example data about behavior patterns.
- The reason of the observed behavior cannot be defined surely, because of the motives, convictions, attitudes and preferences in the background, which are less known. However, this is not relevant in case of the present research, because its goal is not to explore the causes and motives.
- The observation methodology is time-consuming and expensive, as well as, in some cases it can be unethical to observe the behavior of people without their knowledge or permission.

It is argued that in case of the right use of the observation method, valuable information can be collected. This methodology is suitable to complete different questioning methods (e.g. interview or questionnaire).

6.5. The process of data collection – observations

The researcher realized the observations by herself. The observations focused on the interaction between the guide and the tourists, the experience environment provided by the operator and guide, the tourists' level of experience-involvement and the opportunities of customization.

6.5.1. The process of sampling and data collection

The process of sampling in context of the service providers was described at the beginning of the chapter. The observation was held among the tour providers of the sample. As the first step of the data collection a list was received 1-2 weeks before the organization of the planned tours, and the selection happened. By following the schedule, 1-2 tours per day were observed. Various changes could occur, because in some cases only 24 or 48 hours in advance the tour could be cancelled (not enough interest), or the bus seats got all sold.

Table 7: The observational aspects of the tour

Interaction:

- How many times did they ask or talked?
  - *Did they answer any asked questions?*
  - *Could they ask questions?*
- What is the rate between the interactive and non-interactive parts?
- To what extent is the guiding script-like?
  - *Is it theatrical?*
- To what extent does the tour contain informative text / story / narrative / myth / gossip/ personal experience?
- How much engagement / attention does the group show? (the number of interested and uninterested, the level of attention of the tourists (time, physical attention, e.g. turning towards the guide etc.)
- How is the group's mood?
- What is the quality of the dialogue?
  - *Negative or positive*
  - *Pertinent or informative*
- How consumers access information?
  - *Information about the program*
  - *Information about the attraction*
- What is the degree of transparency?

Did the guide inform about the possible risks? Does s/he set any rules?

Experience environment:

- What kind of goods and services do the tourists face during the tour?
  - *How big is their diversity?*
- Is the experience environment themed?
  - *How is it themed?*
- What kind of tools are used during the tour?
  - *for emotional involvement*
  - *for sensorial involvement*
    - Seeing
    - Hearing
    - Smelling
  - *for physical involvement*
  - *for mental involvement*
  - *for social involvement*

Customization:	-	Did some of the program elements change or dismiss because of individual or group request?
	-	Can the tourist decide how much time s/he spends with the consumption of a certain experience? Does the guide limit him/her in it?
	-	Did any customization happen due to the nationality, culture, age or other characteristics of the tourists?
	-	How flexible was the program? Did any spontaneous acts happen?

Source: own compilation

6.5.2. Data fixation

Notes were taken directly during the tours. The observed factors were recorded by the researcher during the tours, sitting on a bus or during the walk. After the tours the notes were transferred into electronic form. The fixation of the data took place right after the tour, the observed factors were fixed in chronological order. Pictures of different moments were also taken during the observations (see Appendix).

6.5.3. Data analysis

The data collection followed a predetermined structure (see Table 7). The analysis was prepared in MS Excel with the help of key concepts and codes. The analysis of the observed data had a descriptive profile.

6.5.4. The researcher's role

During the observations the aim was to blend in the crowd of the group. The guides knew about the role of the researcher. It would be naive to claim that with my presence I did not influence the guide, however, s/he did not know, the purpose of the observation (interaction, customization, etc.). My presence could influenced his / her quality of work, but not the program of the tour or the tools and methods in use.

How does the tour provider influence the consumer experience during the tour? The second research question is related to the consumer experience, which requires a casual research (after the realization of exploratory and descriptive research). Quantitative methodology – a questionnaire was implemented to answer the research question.

7.1. The technique of the methodology in use

The questionnaire is a popular data collection method of social research. Questionnaires are used among respondents, who create a sample from the target population. The questionnaire-type survey is suitable for descriptive research in big target populations, and the data collected is appropriate for explanations (Babbie, 2001). Questionnaire technique can collect data by asking questions from respondents, or asking them to tell their opinions about different standpoints.

According to Babbie (2001) when a questionnaire is designed, various viewpoints have to be kept in mind – the most important ones are the followings:

- the question should be exact and clear,
- a question can ask only about one certain thing,
- the respondent should be competent in answering the question,
- the respondent is willing to answer,
- the question should be relevant for the responder,
- the question should be as short as possible,
- interpretational disfigurations should be avoided.

A pilot data collection is suggested to be performed with the first version of a questionnaire.

The **strengths** of the questionnaire technique are: it is economical, the availability of the data quantity, the standardization ability of the received data. The **weaknesses** of the questionnaire technique are: it is artificial and superficial to a certain level. Other characteristics are that **the validity of the data collected through questionnaires is relatively weak, while their reliability is high** (Babbie, 2001).

7.2.1. Sampling

The process of sampling related to the second question followed Churchill (1995), and it can described as:

- *defining the target population (discrete target population):* the consumers of the destination experience mediators (tour providers) in summer 2013,
- *defining the sampling frame (a list compiled from the elements of the target population, which helps to select the units of the sampling):* the sampling frame was created by tours organized in summer 2013 and the tourists participating on these tours,
- *selecting a sampling procedure:* stratified, systematic and simple random sampling (all tour participants were invited to complete the questionnaire)[4]
- *determining the sample size (influenced by the following factors: how heterogeneous the examined population is, the budget, what is the purpose of the research, how much accuracy is needed):* 80 – 140 questionnaire per tour provider type, the distribution of at least 350 questionnaires in total were planned,
- *selecting the sample elements:* the clientele of the tour providers in summer 2013
    - o observation unit: individual – tourist
- *the timing of sampling and data collection:* 2013, June - August

Realization of interviewer mode of questioning was rejected because of its time- and resource intensity, however, the researcher was present (in cca. 90 % of the cases) during the paper-based data collection, which took place at the end of the tour. The researcher distributed the questionnaires and asked the participants of the tour personally to complete the questionnaire. As the researcher was present, she was able to answer the respondents' questions. In case the researcher was not present, the tour guide distributed and collected the questionnaires.

At first a **preliminary research** was conducted on a **small sample (N=51)** with the proportional involvement of the tour types, in order to clarify the questions, to correct any mistakes (regarding misinterpretation etc.) and to ensure a higher degree of validity.

---

[4] The choice of tours (for questionnaire and observation data collection) was decided by lottery

The sampling was realized on the very same way as in case observations. A list of the tours was received from the tour providers 1-2 weeks in advance, and the choice was made with lottery.

During the sampling procedure the aim was to minimize the researcher's influence. The choice of the tours were random, the participants were all asked to complete the questionnaire at the end of the tour, so everyone had the same possibility to get into the sample. Other researches focusing on tourism experience, used similar sampling methods (e.g. Hosany and Gilbert, 2009; Oh et al., 2007). It can be stated that the sampling procedure corresponded the randomness criterion.

7.2.2. The content development of the questionnaire

The development of the questionnaire involved 3 different tour types, so 3 variation were designed, including only few small differences. The questionnaire also includes variables, which are not directly connected to the hypotheses. From the respondents' perspective it was logical to ask these other questions. Such a variable is satisfaction, or the question at the beginning of the questionnaire: „Why did you choose this tour?" (see questionnaires in the Appendix). These might be used for further empirical analysis, however, it is not presented in the results of the dissertation – only data strongly relating to the hypotheses are analyzed.

7.2.3. The realization of the data collection through questionnaires

In case of small-group and alternative tours (with the collaboration of the guide) the tour usually ended at a suitable place for filling out the questionnaires (for example at benches), which increased the willingness to answer the questions. Most of the times the researcher was present at the tour, which eliminated the problems of timing.

In case of CI and RR bus tours the questionnaires were distributed at the end of the tour, the researcher was present on the whole tour to ensure that the questionnaires are handed out 10 minutes before the end. Only in case of the HoHo tours it was not necessary for the researcher to participate the whole tour at each time.

7.2.4. The language versions of the questionnaire

The questionnaires were designed in English and in Hungarian languages. To minimize the differences between the two language versions, two professional translators were asked to translate the language versions there and back, and then the differences were normalized. The English version of the questionnaire was completed by many nationalities, not only by native English speakers. That is why the questions and answers were put into a simple and clear style.

During the distribution of the questionnaires, each respondent was face to face informed that it is an English language questionnaire (or Hungarian – according to the language of the tour), and also about the goal of the research. The choice of these languages is also reasoned by the researcher's handicap (lack of German, Italian, French, etc. language knowledge). In order to increase the reliability and validity of the results, a question testing the understanding was included (measuring it on a 7-grade scale). Participants marking below point 6 were eliminated from the sample.

7.2.5. The role of the researcher

One of the most important issues about the realization was to find the best occasion for the distribution and completion of the questionnaires. The willingness of completion was partly influenced by the mode how the guide introduced the researcher, and how much s/he personally supported the research. In case of CI the realization was difficult, in case of RR it was easy, while the tour guides of small-group and alternative tour types usually were supporting, too. The main reason behind choosing a paper-based questionnaire (with the presence of the researcher), and realization of an observation, was to increase the reliability and validity of the collected data.

7.3. Scale development

The scale development is a determinative part of the research process, as it defines the content validity of the quantitative research. The content validity has to be ensured before data collection, which means that the variables should represent the real meaning of the construct. With a methodological scale development an important risk – rising from the fact, that the accuracy and reliability of the results are not associated with the validity – can be avoided. The content validity is „a subjective, but a systematic evaluation of the extent to which the content of the construct's scale items represents the measurement task" (Malhotra, 2002: 349). The content validity draws heavily on the researcher's competence, often referred to as expert validity.

Literature review, as the first step of the research, assured the exploration of all those relevant elements of the topic, which are important from the perspective of the research model. As a further step, open-ended questions (qualitative method) and expert validation is suggested as scale development procedures (see Rossiter, 2002). All of these increase the content validity of the constructs and scales.

Scale development suggestions of Churchill (1979) and Rossiter (2002) were taken into consideration. The scale development of the research formed a multi-step process, which had eight major steps:

1. Literature review – definitions and operationalization, the overview of previous researches and existing scales
2. Thesis-proposal defense (expert validation)
3. Qualitative exploratory research – during interviews and observations
4. Netnography – survey of consumer's opinions and experiences
5. Discourse and expert contribution during a PhD research workshop and a professional conference
6. Questionnaire pre-testing
7. Observation and short interviews
8. Expert panel, validation

7.3.1. First step: Literature review

The scales were defined along the variables in the measurement model. After the literature review and the operationalization of the variables, the first draft / list of measurement indicators was formed. In parallel with the operationalization of the definitions and variables, previous scales and related research results were also reviewed. Once the research plan (March 2012) was set up, it was identified that there is no previous research, which would empirically examine the hypothetical relations. This contributes to the academic importance and novelty of the research.

The operationalization of the variables and formation of the hypotheses were realized as the first step of the scale development. The variables and their operationalization are described below.

- **Experience-involvement**

The experience-involvement is the central element of the measurement model. In case of hypotheses H1, H2, H3 it appears as a dependent variable, in case of hypotheses H4 and H5 it appears as an independent variable.

The experience-involvement is defined as active participation of the consumer in the creation and consumption of the experience. Based on the customer experience theory, consumer involvement is possible on four levels: **(1) emotional, (2) sensorial-physical, (3) mental and (4) social level** – this is assumed in case of experience-involvement, too.

A higher level of experience-involvement leads to personal interpretation, the consumer is enriched by mental pictures and meanings by which his / her experience becomes more intense and memorable. The highest level of personal interpretation brings a meaningful experience to the consumer. According to Csíkszentmihályi (1975) the ideal and the highest level of experience is flow, in which a full involvement in an activity leads to a higher state of mind and pleasure. Several scales exist to measure the concept of flow (Mayers, 1978; Jackson et al., 1998; Rheinber et al., 2003), from the 7-point Likert-scale of **Flow Short Scale** (Rheinber et al., 2003) was founded the closest to the measurement model and to the topic of the research in terms of content validity.

The four-realm model of Pine and Gilmore distinguishes 4 basic types of the experience, which was tested by Oh et al. (2007) in tourism, who also developed a scale based on the model. This scale was further tested by Hosany and Gilbert (2009), and also in an earlier research realized by the researcher, although none of these research results have confirmed the content and structure of the model. The model defines four basic types of experience: aesthetic experience, education, entertainment and escapism. Based on the four realm model these experience types jointly assure the optimal experience.

Involvement is not a new construct in marketing literature (see e.g. Rothschild (1984), Laurent and Kapferer (1985), Zaichowsky (1994)). Involvement is interpreted here as a potential of enthusiasm towards a product, service or other activities, due to what it becomes relevant to the individual. In context of leisure and tourism Gusoy and Gavcar (2003), Kyle et al. (2007) and Kaplanidou and Havitz (2010) empirically test and develop a number of various involvement scales. They also view involvement as a degree of enthusiasm and not as involvement in the consumption of a given product, service or activity. Because of different interpretations and validity issues these scales cannot be used in the current research.

Only Zaichowsky's (1999) „**personal involvement inventory**" scale is justified to be applicable in terms of on-site investigations of the experience-involvement.

The above scales with potential validity for the research were added to the list of the scale development.

- **Interaction**

The interaction is an independent (external) variable in hypothesis H1.

Both the concept of experience co-creation and the concept of staged experience emphasize the importance of the interaction between the provider and consumer, but they suggest the implementation of different methods.

According to Prahalad and Ramaswamy (2004) in case of experience co-creation the interaction between the consumers and the companies become the locus of value co-creation. Because the consumers demand different types of interactions, the company should provide a countless variations of the value creation process. The quality of the experience co-creation depends on the interaction infrastructure between the company and the consumer. The interaction between the company and the consumer can start before the travel decision is made, and it can continue after leaving the destination. The interaction is measurable: due to the quantity and quality of the dialogues, consumers' information access (the quantity of the interaction points), transparency and risk sharing.

According to Pine and Gilmore's (1999) concept of staged experience creation, the interaction between the company and the consumer can be described as a drama. The ability of how an experience can engage the individual, and how important is the experience, depends on the extent of the interaction between them.

To adopt to the characteristics of the examined service (sightseeing tours), indicators of interaction were added to the scale development list, not solely on the base of literature review, but mainly based on observations and interviews.

- **Experience environment**

The experience environment is an independent variable in hypothesis H2.

According to the concept of experience co-creation the companies have to innovate the experience environment effectively to enable an optimal diversity of experiences.

The concept of staged experience creation places a great emphasis on formation of the experience environment. According to the concept, the experience environment should be themed, should be filled with cues, which have a positive influence on the experience. It also should contain memorabilia and should engage all the five senses.

Based on the realized literature review there is no scale to measure the experience environment, however the measurement of service environment appears in many researches (e.g. Bitner, 1992; Otto and Ritchie, 1996). These were taken into consideration while creating the list of scale indicators, although the primary results of the interviews and observations had a crucial effect on the development of these indicators, too.

- **Customization**

Customization is an independent variable in hypothesis H3.

Offers allowing customization can be interpreted at two levels: during the consumption, and before the consumption.

During the consumption: how big was the tourist's degree of freedom during the sightseeing tour? Did s/he have the opportunity to change the program or to define how much time s/he wanted to spend with the consumption of a given experience?

` Before the consumption: Could the tourist decide about the program elements? In context of tourism the variable of customization appears in researches of Otto and Ritchie (1996), and Getz (2005) – these were also taken into consideration as possible indicators.

- **The memorability of the experience**

The memorability of the experience is a dependent variable in hypothesis H4. Indicators of memorable experience were examined by Kim et al.'s (2010) exploratory research, which was not realized in on-site conditions, so it might not be valid if applied to the recent research.

The „memorability of tourist experience" scale developed by Oh et al. (2007) with the aim to measure the memorability of the experience, is found to be applicable due to its content validity and methodological fit, which measures the following indicators on a 7-point Likert-scale:

- o I will have wonderful memories from this sightseeing tour.
- o I will remember on many positive things in connection with this sightseeing tour.
- o I won't forget the experiences gained on this sightseeing tour.

- **Authenticity**

Authenticity was examined as a dependent variable in hypothesis H5.

The definition of Wang (1999) was accepted, which distinguishes three types of authenticity: *objective authenticity*, which is related to the authentic origins of the offer, (2) *constructive authenticity*, when authenticity is defined in a symbolic manner, reflecting a personal evaluation, and (3) *existential authenticity*, which is formed by personal feelings arising during the consumption, it derives from the perception of (reaching) an authentic state of being.

This variable is usually measured with qualitative tools, and valid measurement scales are not defined. Therefore the indicators were formed based on literature review and the results of the qualitative researches for the purpose of the preliminary list of scales. The customer survey was found to be applicable only for the measurement of constructive and existential authenticity, while it is not suitable to measure the objective authenticity. This is the consequence of the evaluation's subjective nature, however, it is important to highlight that due to the given profile of the tour the object-related authenticity is rather impossible to interpret.

New valid scales created due to the lack of available scales supports the academic value of the research, however, the scale development process should be performed carefully.

The definition of the construct (latent variable) is the first step of the scale development, in which (1) the rater entity, (2) the object and (3) the attribute need to be defined (Rossiter, 2002). The observed latent variables of the measurement model can be described as:

- **Interaction:** interaction with the service / supplier perceived by the consumers *(rater entity: consumers, object: tour, attribute: service interaction (tour) detected attitude)*
- **Experience environment:** environmental factors perceived by the consumers during the service *(rater entity: consumers, object: service/tour, attribute: the perceived quality of experience environment factors)*
- **Customization:** the customization of the tour perceived by the consumers *(rater entity: consumers, object: tour, attribute: degree of customization)*
- **Experience involvement:** the consumers' degree of involvement into the experience *(rater entity: consumers, object: tour, attribute: degree of experience involvement)*
- **Authenticity:** the genuineness perceived by the consumers based on individual evaluation, and based on the effect on personal state of mind *(rater entity: consumer, object: tour, attribute: to determine the extent of the authenticity based on individual evaluation, and based on the effect on personal state of mind).*
- **Memorability:** the extent of memorability of the consumer experience during the tour *(rater entity: consumer, object: tour, attribute: extent of memorability)*

As next step, the classification of the rater entity, the object and the attribute was performed (see Rossiter, 2002), based on what the reflective nature of the measurement model's variables could be determined.

7.3.2. Second step: Indirect expert validation

Thesis-proposal defense

The thesis-proposal defense, as an indirect expert validation accepted (without any changes) and supported the plan of the new scale formation.

7.3.3. Third step: Qualitative exploratory research

Interviews and observations

The results of in-depth interviews provided useful data for the validation of the measurement model. The observations (some observations were made beforehand the preliminary questionnaire) heavily contributed to the content exploration of independent variables (interaction, experience environment) and to the investigation applicability of existing scale items rooted in theory, secondary data and previous researches.

7.3.4. Fourth step: Netnography

Survey of consumer's opinions and experiences

The netnography makes available an important database of consumers' experiences, while the process of data collection and the sample is not the influenced by the researcher. Due to its target-free nature it is considered to be advantageous compared to other qualitative methods (e.g. interview). In terms of the tourist experience creation, as a complex phenomenon influenced by many factors, this technique is of highlighted importance (Volo, 2009). The netnography is a special type of qualitative content analysis that collects data from the World Wide Web.

The online blogs (and Web 2.0) allow the appearance of consumers' opinion. I chose to analyze Trip Advisor, as an online community page with the most content (in form of reviews) of the examined tour providers. The collected data made possible to explore experience factors, which were important for previous consumers to express, to share and to form an opinion about. The netnography examined the entries between the 1st of November 2012 and the 30th of March 2013 with the goal to explore the practical manifestation of the latent variables and to create valid indicators.

7.3.5. Fifth step: Discourse and expert contribution

The development of the scales and questionnaire continued on a PhD workshops and on an international conference. On the PhD workshop, led by Prof. Steward Clegg, the participating doctoral students presented and discussed their researches. The recent research plan and the measurement model gained support accompanied with valuable remarks and criticism. Helpful suggestions for further development were received, from which I would highlight the scale development step of short interviews.

On the *3rd International Research Forum on Guided Tours* international conference in 4-6th April 2013, a lecture presenting the first results of the qualitative research was realized, and the content development of the scales were discussed. A positive feedback from the audience (around 30 participants with academic and/or professional background) was received. Some changes in the content were suggested by one expert, Dr. Rosemary Black, who shared her opinion and proposed few modifications.

As the next step, the preliminary questionnaire was finalized and realized consequently. The short interviews made with participants of the tours took place during the preliminary data collection and questionnaire testing. This solution (2in1) was preferred due to lack of time and material resources. Because of methodological deliberations on-site data collection was chosen.

7.3.6. Sixth step: Questionnaire testing

Preliminary data collection

Between the 17th of April and the 5th of May 2013 (in 3 weeks) 51 questionnaires were completed. The test examined the lucidity of the questions, the willingness of completion, and the consumer-friendly quality of the questionnaire (the length, the form and clarity of the questions and response options), and it investigated the organizational and realization issues of the procedure. The clarity of the questions produced a 6.26 average, which can be judged as good, the value was lower than 6 only in 4 cases. The consumer-friendly quality was confirmed, as from the 51 completed questionnaires only 3 found it difficult to understand – which is an acceptable error rate. The willingness to complete the questionnaire was also favorable.

The lack of financial and other resources meant an obstacle in testing the scales and questionnaires on a larger sample. From methodological point of view it is not considered to be appropriate to involve individuals not in the role of a tourist into the research – the experience could become distorted, the answers and results would not serve the validity of the scales (see Hair et al., 2009).

7.3.7. Seventh step: Observation and short interviews

The observations during the test questionnaires provided additional information to complete the structure and content of the scales and questionnaires. During the tour and after the test questionnaires, the researcher tried to ask tour participants about the factors that have determined or influenced their tour experience. As the researcher did not have the possibility to involve a larger sample under organized conditions, free, case-level, interviewer-type data collection (short interviews) were performed on a smaller sample. During the test questionnaire and the observations in this phase 18 evaluated answers were collected from the participants of the tour, between 17th April and 5th May 2013. Based on these results the following conclusions about the influencing factors of tourist experience were determined (the number of mentionings are indicated in brackets): *theme (5), nice guide (5), entertaining tour guiding (4), passionate tour guiding (3), interesting information (3), importance of surprise factor (2), weather (2), quality of the bus (1), good mood (1).*

7.3.8. Eighth step: Expert panel

Before the short interviews the first expert validation took place which was focusing on the content of the scales – with the participation of Dr. Melanie Smith, Dr. Noémi Kulcsár and Dr. László Puczkó. Some elements were skipped because of methodological consideration, and only those elements were added to the new scale, which received at least 2 supports from the 3 experts. The indicators of the scales are listed in the Appendix.

The scales of the research can be viewed as measurement tools. I chose to order interval type of scales to the variables due to their metrical features. This is justified by the related researches, but methodological deliberations also support the application of 7-point Likert-scale. The interval type (differential) scale indicates how big the difference between two scale points is.

Based on methodological consideration the „don't know" category in the questionnaire was introduced as an answer option, to avoid the respondents' choice of the mean value as from „psychological zero" opinions (see Rossiter, 2002). Additionally, next to the middle 4th point on the 7-point scale, the answer option „decidedly neutral" was indicated and highlighted to eliminate such a possible, negative impact on the validity.

Wherever it was possible (in case of variables: interaction and experience-involvement) contrary adjectives were indicated at the two extremes of the scale, for better clarity and consumer friendliness (similar to Zaichowsky's scale).

8. THE RESULTS OF QUALITATIVE RESEARCH

The goal of the qualitative research was to investigate the extent to which the tour providers in Budapest apply the experience-centric approach regarding their methods and management perspective: how do they view consumers, what are the cornerstones of their strategic thinking, and how do they apply these principles when designing and executing various work processes. Beyond that, the research aimed to explore the value-creating process in its entirety, thus interviews were made with not only managers, but also with guides (i.e. those directly interacting with consumers). Therefore the research, implemented with the qualitative research technique, examines two different subjects with different roles and tasks with the help of two different questionnaires.

Although the two questionnaires were variants in their length and content, they completed each other. To get a deeper exploration and more comprehensive exploration of the topic, besides the methodology of the in-depth interview, and the conversations with the employees taking part in the service-providing process, observation was also put into practice as the next step of the research. The focus of the observation was on the process of the tour as the central element of the service. The three separate, nevertheless connected research elements aimed to shed light on the following question.

- **How and to what extent does the experience-centric approach – particularly the staged experience concept and the experience co-creation concept – determine the management approach and service provision of tour providers?**

The question is exploratory and descriptive at the same time. Collected data is analyzed through the **research sub-questions** formed by the **Conceptual Frame of Experience-centric Management** (Table 5), which can be seen in the next subsection. This way, certain elements of the framework will fuse into the sub-questions along the content coherence. The introduction of the results will not be presented in the order of the interview structure, but following the order of the analysis criteria and the research sub-questions.

(1) What is the role of tourist experience on the market of tourism?

The tour providers unanimously agree with the statement that on the consumer side, travelling is increasingly about experiences, fulfillment and rejuvenation. They are putting emphasis on:

- to provide a novel experience (DIS),[5]
- to treat experience as value (EU),
- to focus on experience offers (PC).

(2) What kind of service providing and value creating process would be required to fulfill the consumers' need? Are there any opportunities offered to consumers for the active participation? Is the consumers' deeper involvement in experience in favor of the service providers? To what degree is a tour interactive?

Based on the results from the interviews and observations, during the service provision the standard **small-group tour providers** are measurably consumer- and experience-focused including **the quality of interaction,** as well as, the **involvement and activity of the tour participants. The size of the group** is a determinative factor.

Although the bus tour providers offer opportunities for interaction, they do not support it, so **their tours are not interactive.** In addition, **they are not even trying to facilitate the involvement during the tour** (except RR), however active attendance is offered for participants.

Regarding **alternative tours,** it is ascertained that the tours of each service provider have distinct interactivities. Interactivity is not only realized through dialogues, but with the help of questions and tasks as well. They pay outstanding attention to the **involvement in experience** beyond interactivity.

Results have revealed these involvement stimulating tools:

- stimulating dialogues (HL)
- brainstorming tasks (UQ, BU)
- collective knowledge-creation, community experience (HL, BU)
- game (BU, UQ, RR)

---

[5] Example: "DIS" and other abridgements mark data of in-depth interviews with a certain tour provider (see Chapter 6), its derived from their names.

- involvement with the help of drawing (IG)
- keeping the attention (interesting stories, with sense of humor) (IG)
- usage of social media (BU, IG, HL)
- sensorial stimulus – e.g. music, lyrics, food (FRE, DIS)
- strengthen the visualization in terms of the journey through times – with contemporary pictures, maps, videos (IG, UQ, HL, BU)

(3) To what extent and how do the experience-centric, knowledge-intensive value-creating business processes manifest themselves?

In non-hierarchical organizations (alternative and most of small-group tour providers) knowledge-sharing is emphasized while in moderately hierarchical organizations (bus tour providers and DIS) the process is centralized by a top-down initial, which does not have a positive effect on knowledge-intensive business processes.

(4) How and to what extent do they usually estimate the consumers' expected fields of interest and experiences anticipated by consumers? Is this knowledge utilized during the course of service and value creation processes?

The consumers' expected fields of interest are explored just **before the initiation of the tour** in the case of **small-group tours.** Furthermore it is possible to vary the program on-demand during the tour (except the CI). The **bus tour providers** without an exception have already tried to make a survey about the preference of guests and guest satisfaction. In order to satisfy the guests, they vary and create programs according to experiences of tour providers, but during the tour **there is no chance to change or modify as the programs have a fix structure and content.** From the aspect of tour guides: few tour guides pay attention to the cultural diversity of participants and form the guiding according to the given situation (RR-Guide 1, CI-Guide 1, FRE-Guide 2).[6] For some of the tour guides **it's important to create an elated atmosphere in the group** (DIS-Guide2, FRE-Guide2). In the case of alternative tours, the special theme of the tour predestinates the participants' field of interest, but consumers' needs and ideas are also important for them.

---

[6] Example: RR-Guide 1 – „RR" refers to the tour provider's name, "Guide1" refers to the data collection of the first interview with tour guide of RR.

(5) What kind of experience does the tour provide? What kind of emphasis is on the provided experience during the tour? How much is the service provision experience-centric?

The personalized atmosphere of the tour could be assured by the small-size group– the small-size group tour providers limit the group size. CI uses the tools of experience management for the purpose of distinguishing itself from the competitors (unique products offer special experience), at the same time experience is treated as an added supplement of the product.

HoHo tours provide **plenty of freedom** for the participants. 'The cheapest and the most successful way of getting acquainted with the city' is the promise for the experience of HoHo sightseeing tour (PC) – it means a certain kind of rational approach. RR tour supposes that beside the 'splashing' experience due to the special technological solution, experience deriving from the sightseeing is just additional, nevertheless the quality of services are highlighted.

In case of alternative tours, learning is the main experience, but emotional and community experience also play important roles. IG supposes that for a citizen of Budapest, a tour is a more memorable experience because what is shown to them is totally new or they have only known it from a different aspect – which means that the experience factor of the tour is higher because of the surprise and amusement.

Tour guides express the experience they are striving to create in different ways, and they also prove them with the main experience-dimensions stated by the literature:

- Unique experience – *„Get something what was never experienced before"* (DIS-Guide1)
- Creating a dialogue – *„let the guest talk"* (BU-Guide1)
- Personal customization – *„satisfying personal needs"* (FRE-Guide2)
- Emotional involvement – *„reach them"* (BU-Guide1) *„it's important that they laugh, it doesn't matter if they cry sometimes."* (FRE-Guide1)
- Unforgettable experience (FRE-Guide1) (BU-Guide2)
- Personal connection with the tour guide (FRE-Guide1)
- Experience of discovery, *„....not the tour guide should tell."* (BU-Guide1)
- Uplifted mood *"...when they leave, their eyes should shine"* (DIS-Guide2)

(6) What kind of innovations are introduced? How and to what extent does the main role of experience-themes appear in product development?

Small-group tour providers are reported to be the most experience-oriented and the most creative in field of innovation. They are the most innovative – e.g. new experience-themes like Ghost Tour, a street theater performance as a sightseeing tour were introduced. The tours of DIS provide a complex promise of experience since several experience factors are usually mixed – gastronomy, walking, shopping, break at a host location etc.

Even if product developments of bus tour providers are realized in order to enhance experience, they cannot be called innovations focusing on consumer experience themes; they should rather be referred to as developments aiming the improvement of service quality and consumers' experience.

Although DIS tours are said to be complex from the aspect of experience promises, its feasibility and rentable nature are highlighted during the innovation. Several tour guides are referring to this fact as the main obstacle of experience-centric perspective.

At **alternative tour providers**, the theme is invented by own research or through an outside reference. They claim to never receive any theme ideas from the audience. The participants have the opportunity to add their own experience and knowledge to the tour, which presupposes a sort of **co-created experience.** Furthermore, the first-handed information and memories also enhance the **authenticity**. The development of the product is usually realized through brainstorming among the members of the organizing team, the main question is what the public is the most interested in. *'It is important to offer an interesting theme, ...in which people are interested enough, which they will come for, which can be explored in a determined area and can be filled with interesting stories.' (UQ).*

(7) Do the participants meet the local community during the tour? Do the locals play any part in the tour?

In the case of standard sightseeing tours involvement of locals and meeting with the members of the community are not included in the program.

During bus tours, tour providers do not give any opportunities to participants to practice this kind of activity. Since the tour can be customized to a great extent, it is possible that the tourists are making friends with locals after getting off the HoHo bus.

Sometimes locals or people of the visited site join in the BU tour spontaneously. The aim and the mission of UQ is to blend into the local community's life as much as they can. An important coefficient is connected to the authenticity: the places visited by alternative tour providers are thought to be less visited (or it is impossible to get there individually – UQ, IG, BU, HL), in this way they provide insight into the secrets of local lifestyle.

(8) What makes tour guiding good? Do the tour providers consider the narrative to be important? How are the elements of narrative involved in the tour?

To the question of what makes **tour guiding good**, the most consistent opinions have highlighted these points:

- the **importance of collective experience development** *(„if tour guiding is not an obligation, rather a pleasure" (FRE-Guide1)," if it is done with love and passion" (BU-Guide1), „ the biggest secret is that I love doing it,... if it's boring for the tour guide, it must be boring for the participants, too" (DIS-Guide2))*,
- *development of pleasant group atmosphere („walls must be demolished, contacts and good atmosphere must be created" (DIS-Guide2), „establishing a positive vibe is crucial" (DIS-Guide2), „making contacts with the guests " (RR-Guide1) (DIS-Guide2))*,
- **to acquire the consumers' viewpoints** *(„I get right inside the part of the tourist" (RR-Guide2) (DIS-Guide1), „The tourist's experience is important not the experience which the tour guide thinks is important" (CI-Guide1), „insight into human nature is needed: what the tourist wants" (DIS-Guide1), „to get acquainted with the group" (IG-Guide1), „to treat people well" (PC))*,
- **a humor** *(„little moments that make them smile" (RR-Guide1)," to put humorous stories in it" (RR-Guide2), humor (DIS-Guide1) (FRE-Guide2),"they need help to get amazed" (DIS-Guide2))*,
- **Interesting stories, narrative storytelling** *("history is told in an entertaining and spontaneous way through well-tried stories (FRE-Guide2)", "telling gossips and interesting stories" (IG-Guide2).*

The recorded tour guiding of EU and PC make the facts more colorful with narrative parts (EU-Obs.) (PC-Obs.)[7], and RR tour guiding also adopt these elements. (RR-Obs.) According to CI, narratives, personal reference of tour guides, and story-telling are all important since they are valued by the guests. However, in CI there are no special terms or expectations for tour guides to build personal narrative into the tour. At the same time in RR, tour guides are expected to tell stories, interesting facts in a humorous way. In the case of small-size tours, narrative style and personal stories are common (DIS-Obs.2-3, FRE-Obs.1-2, BB-Obs.1-2).[8]

Referring to urban legends, stories and gossips typify the tours of alternative tour providers; performance is usually realized in a narrative style. UQ draws a parallel

---

[7] Obs. refers to data from observations

[8] Obs.1.-2. – the numbers refers to the sequence of the observed tour

between experience and myths: *„It is important for us to be able to transmit experience, stories, legends, which are really beloved by people."*

(9) Consumers co-create value with other consumers and service providers while they remain active in searching and creating value. Products and services are parts of the experience environment where the co-creation of the value takes part. Products and services are merely intermediaries of experience developed by individuals and communities.

Based on the definition **small-group tour providers** confirmed that the management approach they implement is close to the approach of co-created value. They believe that this approach derives from the nature of small-sized group tours. According to them, tourism should be about co-creation of value, customized and authentic experiences. *„Tourists would rather expect to feel emotions than acquire knowledge."(DIS)* This feeling is attributable to the result of value co-creation. That is why the transmission of knowledge during the tour should happen in an experience-focused and entertaining way. So experience *„does not only depend on the program, but on the tour guide who should transmit the knowledge in an entertaining way."* *(DIS).* CI approves both aspects, but believes that only the firm can create value.

EU does not agree with it, while RR only does so partly.

Alternative tour providers only partly agree with the items of value co-creation. According to them, value is developed by tour providers, and the guest is only a recipient.

(10) Have they perceived the existence of consumer community?

None of the service providers have perceived the existence of consumer community. They are not even that much interested in it because of the tourists' temporary and generally non-recurring stay – except of alternative tour consumers.

The clientele of **alternative tour organizers** is divided into two homogenous groups – the one of elderly age-group between 50-65, and the one of young intellectuals around 30. Since the theme of the tour is specific, their fields of interest could be said to be roughly similar. Until now none of the service providers have strived to raise a clientele or have even perceived its existence around them. Although they have followers on websites, and the number of their followers who participate frequently in alternative sightseeing tours keeps increasing, there is no significant interaction or any kind of organization among them. IG, BU and HL declared that they would be happy to develop a clientele, but they have not put any further effort into it. Small-group tour providers also practice this kind of clientele building.

(11) Do they cooperate with other tour providers?

All in all it can be stated that in the case of examined service providers, there is no remarkable networking with other market players, there is only a basic, elementary and incompact form of it. However, they put a great emphasis on strengthening their relations with their subcontractors and intermediators because of their business interests.

Without exception the alternative tour providers have stressed that they believe in partnership. In spite of having put forward the theory of partnerships, alternative tour providers do not cooperate and network with each other, although there have been some attempts previously.

(12) Do they involve consumers in the determination of unique value? Is co-created value highlighted in terms of participation and interaction?

All inspected standard small-group and alternative tour providers are trying to create a **unique value offer** on the market, although most of them have indicated that there is a danger of copying. All of them have unique product offers or at least additional products which distinguishes them on the market.

Consumers have a say in the matter of forming the tour schedule of only HoHo type products (and during private tours), so in this case, conditions are given to the strict value co-creation, in the course of which the consumer creates the value from the elements of experience environment partly developed by service providers, who also support them throughout the whole value creation process (the latter is not always fulfilled regarding to the inspected service providers). Although the tour type makes the customization possible, it does not support the involvement and value co-creation, for this reason it cannot be called experience-centric.

Based on observations during segway tours and small-group bicycle and walking tours, involvement is **much more represented** than in the case of bus tours. During the course of tours, guests are given the opportunity to freely decide upon each point of the tour schedule. Tours are not strictly time-bound, they sometimes last thirty minutes longer as the time spent at some stops is determined by the guests' needs.

The idea of co-creation of the value appears in the approach of FRE service providers in which the **tour guide's experience** is also important, so in the **co-creation process of the value**, value is developed for not only 2, but 3 persons- the guest, the tour guide and the tour provider: *„We would like to involve everyone, nobody should be bored... this type is the preferred by tour guides"* (FRE).

During **alternative tours** participants are usually encouraged to enhance the value of the tour by giving feedbacks and adding extra information. This type of **knowledge-sharing** results in the co-creation of value between the audience and the tour. Alternative tour organizers do not only add interactive elements to the tour, but brainstorming tasks as well. **Making the participants proactive** encourages the co-creation of values.

(13) How and to what extent does the interaction appear in access, transparency, risk-benefits and dialogues relevant to the co-creation of values?

Small-group and bus tour providers are not keen on keeping in touch with former guests: *„because who has once seen the city, will not ever come back to see it again."*(EU) In the case of non-HoHo type bus tours, the communication preceding the tour mainly occurs through mediators. Mediators and small-size tour providers regard online guest opinions and feedbacks prominently important on account of the high rate of internet-based orientation – for instance on TripAdvisor or on GetYourGuide.

Active contact with Hungarian guests is a typical characteristic of the alternative tour providers, which tend to keep a customer database, although it is varying how much they can benefit from it – clientele program (IG), newsletter (HL, BU), questionnaires for guests' opinion (BU, IG). The communication before or after alternative tours takes place on social networking sites, although local journalists often write articles about the more intriguing tours.

Tour providers are striving for the access, transparency, so they use diverse online and offline communication channels. Informing about risk-sharing happens in case of special (e.g. self-guided) vehicles (bicycle, segways).

8.3. Investigation of aspects of staged experience

(14) Drama should be the focal metaphor of business. Company is viewed as a "theatre", workers are "actors", customers are the "audience" or "guests", the physical environment is the "stage", and the "show" is performed by service providers.

Small-group tour providers definitely do not agree with the "drama" concept. According to FRE, this concept is only true for the Ghost Tour, while even in the case of street-theatre-like tours, formation of co-created experiences is the most crucial one.

Opinions of HoHo tour providers are varied: PC does not agree, while EU admits that drama is the right metaphor, since those working in the tourism industry are all playing a role.

Alternative tour providers agree with the fundamental assumption of staged experience creation to a certain degree:

„ Actually, the way we are doing it... city walk is a performance, a drama" (BU)

„It is true that the city is the stage and settings, but the other assumptions are not: we are not actors, we are also interested in real life." (HL)

„The company is the equivalent of the theatre, but the experience does not come to life without an audience.... At the same time, experience should be produced by the company." (IG)

(15) To guarantee an optimal experience, four realms have to be realized: (1) entertainment, (2) learning, (3) aesthetics, and (4) escapism?

Among small-group tour providers, only one service provider (FRE) agrees fully with this theory. **The other opinions evidence different approaches**:
- Optimal experience can be mainly reached through entertainment. (BB)
- Escapism is not necessarily needed for the optimal experience. (DIS)

Bus tour providers have also declared differently:
- The 4R model is not necessarily true, it depends on where one is, e.g. on the beach there is no learning, but on a bus learning is important. These two experiences are different. All the four types of experience are presented in services provided by them.
- On HoHo tours, optimal experience is assured by cultural experience and learning rather than entertainment. However, the list of coupons which is included in the ticket, ensures further types of services and experiences. (PC)
- The more complex is a tourist attraction, the better it will be (RR)

All alternative tour providers have had different opinions:

- Regarding the optimal tourist experience, BU believes that escapism is the most important, which also means that *„non-locals become locals"* during an alternative tour.
- According to HL, community experience is also important besides the four experience realms.
- In the approach of IG, learning is not necessarily needed for an optimal tourist experience, although they focus on it a lot.
- As UQ believes, optimal tourist experience has a strong subjective nature, it has a different meaning for everyone (e.g. different for an engineer or a 12-year-old). Furthermore, it is viewed as a complicated and complex entity that's dimensions cannot be determined separately.

(16) Can sustainable competitiveness be reached only by creating unique and memorable experiences?

All service providers agree that a unique and memorable experience is significant.

Alternative tours not only aim to be unforgettable, but also focus on enhancing personal development (BU). What makes a tour unique is the tour guide by putting inside his/her own personality, and reflecting to the audience and its needs (HL). Memorability is the prime indicator of the quality of the tour: *„ When the guest comes home, he can talk about it [the tour], it remains in him,…[it is] mainly moments."* *(IG).*

Methods and tools which try to assure the uniqueness of the tours:
- innovative product development (CI, RR, DIS)
- new ideas in terms of additional services and product packages (PC, EU)
- cooperation in partnerships (HL, BU, CI)

Methods and tools which try to provide the memorability of the tours:
- surprise factor (HL)
- group photo at the end of the tour or during it (FRE, CI)
- more sensorial stimulus – e.g. using pictures, visualization (IG, UQ)
- making themes, theatrical performance/wearing costumes (IG, FRE)
- reading quotes (BU, HL, IG, UQ)

(17) Does the most valuable form of experience only entertain or also provide the opportunity for personal development?

BU and IG merely aims their tours to lead towards personal development. At the same time, others highlight that intensive (HL) and unforgettable (UQ) experiences can lead towards individual learning. IG tours aim to change people's perspective: to make them more responsible citizens, and to show them how beautiful the city is.

(18) Does thematization typify the experience?

Having examined the themed experience surrounding of tours, it can be stated that RR tours are thematized to the biggest extent from all service providers. Some CI tours also have themes – they are usually organized in small groups (e.g. Dicta-tour). The above mentioned Ghost Tour of FRE is a thematic sightseeing tour, too, it is a street theater show with an outstanding performance starring a guide dressed up as a ghost (FRE-Obs.3).

The tours of alternative tour providers are less thematic, although few attempts have been made; but recently they decided to eliminate this tour element because of organizational circumstances and costs (IG-Obs.2). In each alternative tour, several tools are used not only for theming, but also in order to increase authenticity and enhance involvement, for instance: portfolios and tablets.

(19) Is experience creation standardized by the tour provider?

Due to its nature, HoHo sightseeing tours have the highest standardization rate because of the recorded tour guiding. *This kind of automatization cannot be characterized by the co-staged experience concept (Prahalad, 2004), as neither the resulting degree of freedom nor the self-service do necessarily result in experience co-creation.* HoHo tour providers' opinions are diverse, while EU believes that recorded tour guiding is preferred by the guests. According to PC, live tour guiding has a higher experience factor so that is why one of their tour lines remained to employ a live guiding.

According the interviewed HoHo tour providers, there is no detailed behavioral or guideline instructions at the company which would control employees' work routine, although they operate with many hosts/hostesses and street salesmen (CI-Obs., PC-Obs.). Permanent trainings for employees are provided by both service providers. In the case of RR, we can state that tour guiding is standardized, but personal traits can be built into it (RR-Obs.1-2-3).

Regarding DIS and FRE, tour routes are mainly set; documentation is provided for the content of the guiding, which can be used in a flexible way by tour guides. „*The more we are, the more different ways how we do it, everybody is different, there is no receipt, someone is more humorous, someone has more serious or easygoing style. Any*

of these could be great for the tourists – there is no certain way that everyone likes."
(FRE).

However, CI tour guides are free to decide about the content of the tour (CI-Obs.1-2-3), in addition one third of the tour routes and stopovers depends on their decision beside the main stopovers known from the program of the tour. They trust the tour guide's creativity which reduces the standardization factor.

On closer examination of **alternative tour providers** different working processes and conceptions have been revealed. First one is when an expert of the given subject who set up the tour, guide it as well. IG and BU are not searching for tour guides, they rather look for professionals: landscape architects, litterateurs, historians etc., who has broad knowledge and professional experience in the certain field, and they are able to guide a tour about it. Hereby it also endangers that the expert's tour guiding and presenter skills are not that much good – as they are not professional guides. According to IG, the technique can be acquired easier than the knowledge. Second case is, e.g. in case of HL other members of the team help the tour guide to set up the tour. Separation of the roles (tour guide and tour constructor) can be observed here. It can favor the tour guiding quality, if the tour was guided by qualified tour guide with good presenter skills.

UQ has already gone further: separated the content and structure formation of the tour schedule, and the realization of the tour. The content and structure construction of the tour is the management's responsibility; they also hold training tours for the tour guides, which contains a communication training.

(20) To what extent are scenarios important to the tour providers?

RR applies scenarios in order to determine what the tour guide should say or do. The content (text) was prepared by professional authors and tour guides, but all tour guides can present it in their own style. At IG tours scenarios are also written – during the tour participants do not perceive the guiding spontaneous at all (IG-Obs.1-2). HL applies a kind of a scenario which allows other guides to lead the tour. At BU this occurs only in inevitable situations. All the tours of UQ have a fixed base, fixed route, fixed syllabus and certain things which have to be said, but, because the content of the tour is more detailed than the time frame, the tour guide can decide and interpret *"those parts s/he is more interested about personally, the ones that s/he can present with more genuinely"* (UQ).

(21) To what extent is it important that the tour guides build their personality traits into their role?

The more personality traits applies the tour guide during the tour, the better and the more personalized the experience will become: „...*The more they can give from themselves, the more can be transmitted.*"(UQ). At RR, tour guides are expected to be friendly, easy-going, loose and informal. Individual personality traits show up from both parties during the tour, as the tour schedule can be flexible and customized (BB-Obs.1-2). During individual and small-group tours, tourists determine what they want to hear, so the guide's reflection on the audience's requirements is needed. (UQ, HL).

(22) Are metaphors of drama and storytelling applied during the tour?

Only Ghost Tour is based on metaphors of drama and storytelling (FRE-Obs.3), although background music and other narrative parts appear in recorded tour guiding of PC (PC-Obs.), in addition RR also stages the moment of river splash and debarkation with sound effects in order to enhance experience. During alternative tours, dramatic and narrative effects are reached mostly by reading contemporary quotes to increase the experience-involvement. (BU-Obs.2, HL-Obs.2, IG-Obs.2).

8.4. Summary of the results

After the analysis and evaluation of the results, the three types of studied tour providers have been compared along experience-centric perspective and its two theoretical concepts. Figure 12 presents and compares that in what extent the experience-centric management concept and value creation processes of the tour provider types are experience-centric, and whether their experience-centric perspective is characterized by the staged or co-created experience approach.

Based on the conclusion and collation of the qualitative results it can be stated that **small group tour providers and alternative tour providers** are characterized with the experience-centric perspective to the biggest extent. While in the area of management and operations of small group tour providers almost exclusively the approach of experience co-creation appears, in case of alternative tour providers the approach of staged experience creation and experience co-creation are both applied. The management perspective of both types are experience-centric, however, some fields and management aspects are still seeking development in this direction.

Big group and bus type tour providers are characterized with the use of experience-centric approach in lower degree. The hindering facilities of acquiring experience-centric approach are arising from the specific features of the tour type (size of the group, the means of the transport causing passivity). However they try to manage these hindering facilities with an aim to provide a better experience. They perceive experience rather as a product supplementary. In their case there are more fields (in areas of product development and operations), which would need development to be more experience-centric. From the discussed approaches staged experience concept is the most typical here, which is especially applied by one of the suppliers (RR). In case of HoHo type tour providers the concept of experience co-creation offers untapped opportunities and suitable methods of development.

Figure 11: Comparison of the degree of experience-centric approaches of tour provider types

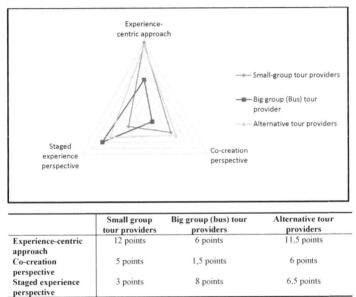

	Small group tour providers	Big group (bus) tour providers	Alternative tour providers
Experience-centric approach	12 points	6 points	11,5 points
Co-creation perspective	5 points	1,5 points	6 points
Staged experience perspective	3 points	8 points	6,5 points

Source: own compilation

The summary of the results was realized based on the analytical framework. Elements of each concept have been evaluated numerically, depending on how much they typify the specific tour provider type. The results of the matrix based on relative comparison allows answering the assumptions of the qualitative research.

- **Assumption 1: The experience-centric approach is mostly characteristic of small-scale tour providers.**

Referring to the results, the assumption has been accepted.

- **Assumption 2: In the case of alternative tour providers, the experience co-creation concept is the ruling principle.**

Assumption has been accepted, however it has to be mentioned that co-created experience methods are not much ahead of the application of staged experience creation methods.

- **Assumption 3: The staged experience concept is not predominant among any of the tour providers.**

Results have contradicted the assumption, as the experience-centric approach of big group (bus) tour providers principally manifests itself in methods and concepts of staged experience.

The data collection of the questionnaire took place between 26th June and 15th September 2013. In total 382 questionnaires were completed on 42 tours. The data collection was followed by the electronic recording of offline questionnaires using MS Office/Excel software, while questionnaires were tagged with numbers in order of controllability and to filter potential errors.

During raw data clearance the questionnaires filled barely or apparently negligibly were extracted – at the end 348 questionnaires remained in the sample. Missing values were refilled with the help of AMOS software through indicator imputation – this procedure provides the most reliable data. Its condition is the presence of a maximum 10% proportion of missing values in the data set (Hair et al., 2009) – this criterion was fulfilled.

The condition of analysis of the structural (theoretical) model is that the latent variables must be unidimensional, reliable and valid. Therefore, as first, exploratory factor analysis (EFA) took place to ensure the principle of unidimensionality.

9.1. Exploratory factor analysis

Exploratory factor analysis was executed by SPSS 20.0 software. Principal Component analysis method with Varimax rotation and Kaiser normalization was applied to reveal experience dimensions. First, all the indicators of the measurement models appeared in the exploratory factor analysis. Certain latent variables separated along dimensions, - while the multidimensionality of variables such as authenticity, experience involvement and experience environment was excelled. In case of these variables (second-order latent variables), creation of second-order scales is required. The differentiation of second-order latent variables is justified by the result of exploratory factor analysis: when it creates several non-orthogonal factors within the given variable. Ideally, if the factor indicators are summarized, principle of unidimensionality will be fulfilled during the exploratory factor analysis (Ping, 2004). This has been accomplished.

This was followed by the execution of the exploratory factor analysis, focusing separately on (1) the influence of service providers (independent variables), and (2) the dependent variables: involvement into the experience (as the indicator of experience intensity), and (3) the experience outcome (memorability and the perception of authenticity). KMO-values were optimal in all cases.

Having examined the **influence of service provider,** indicators with low communality (<0.5), haven't accomplishing the statistical preconditions, were deleted in accordance with the procedure. The outcome of running calculations has revealed the following structure beside the biggest proportion of variance explained (70.8%) (Table 8).

Table 8: Revealed factors of the service provider effect

Factor	Code	Indicator	Factor-weight
1. factor: Interaction	interest2	The presentation of the tour guide was interesting.	.776
	involv2	The presentation of the tour guide was involving.	.690
	passion2	The presentation of the tour guide was passionate.	.745
	infomtv2	The presentation of the tour guide was informative.	.831
	entert2	The presentation of the tour guide was entertaining.	.803
	trustw2	Information on the tour was trustworthy.	.748
2. factor: Interactive experience environment	durinfo6	I received clear information (orientation) on the tour	.765
	content6	I liked the content of the tour	.733
	hear6	I could hear the guiding properly	.736
3. factor: Organizational experience environment	transp6	I'm satisfied with the quality of the transport	.681
	schedu6	The schedule (timing) of the tour was precise	.707
	secur6	I felt secure during the tour.	.791
	comfort6	I felt (physically) comfortable during the tour.	.806
4. factor: Customization	sponta6	The tour contained spontaneous program elements	.790
	choice6	I felt I had a chance of choice during the tour	.897
	control	I felt the I have control over my experience	.823

Source: own construction (2013)

As result of the examination of experience involvement construct, indicators which have not accomplished the statistical preconditions because of low communality (<0.5) were deleted in accordance with the procedure. The outcome of running calculations has revealed the following structure beside the biggest proportion of variance explained (66.7%) (Table 9).

Table 9: Revealed factors of experience-involvement

Factor	Code	Indicator	Factor weight
1. factor: General involvement	enjoy3	The tour was exciting.	.712
	excit3	The tour was enjoyable.	.726
	inspir3	The tour was inspiring.	.614
	engag3	The tour was engaging.	.623
	surpr3	Tour was surprising.	.540
	learn3	I learned a lot during the tour.	.694
	thoupro3	The tour was thought-provoking.	.464
	intere3	The tour is interesting.	.717
	morelea3	I would like to learn more about it.	.535
	visuatt3	The tour is visually attractive.	.639

2. factor: Flow-level involvement	uniq3	The tour is unique.	.580
	valuea3	The tour is valuable for me.	.728
	meaninf3	The tour meant a lot for me.	.696
	getway3	The tour helped me to get away from it all	.739
	active3	The tour made me feel active.	.661
	loststor3	I lost myself in the story.	.688
3. factor: Social involvement	compot3	I enjoyed the company of others in the group.	.851
	gratmos3	There was a good group atmosphere on the tour.	.759
	grintera3	The group interacted well with each other	.848
	intergui3	I had rich interaction with the guide	.633

Source: own construction (2013)

Examining the **outcome variables of the experience** (memorability and perception of authenticity), indicators not accomplishing the statistical preconditions because of low communality (<0.5) were deleted in accordance with the procedure. The outcome of running calculations has revealed the following structure beside the biggest proportion of variance explained (76.8%) (Table 10):

Table 10: Revealed factors of experience outcome variables

Factor	Code	Indicator	Factor-weight
1. factor: Constructive authenticity	sighaut6	Most of the sights seemed authentic / genuine	.778
	reflocal6	The tour was a good reflection of local life and culture	.831
	expaut6	My experience seemed to be authentic	.801
2. factor: Existential authenticity	relate6	I experienced something which I could relate to	.573
	persdev6	It contributed to my personal development	.767
	leamysf6	I learned about myself during the tour	.825
3. factor: Memorability	memo6	I will have wonderful memories about this tour	.862
	remem6	I will remember many positive things about this tour	.843
	forget6	I will not forget my experience at this tour	.832

Source: own construction (2013)

Authenticity and memorability, as the **dependent, outcome factors** of the structural model, are separated appropriately in the measurement model in the result of the exploratory factor analysis. Authenticity appears to be a second order scale with two factors. In their content they separate from each other based on the theory and the initially formed scale-items – as *constructive* and *existential authenticity* factor. Indicators of memorability are organized in one factor, so it strengthened the validity of the already existing scale.

Then **internal consistency** of factor structures followed, which proved the content reliability of the scale. In case of exogenous variables, **Cronbach-alpha values** were between 0.794 and 0.903, in case of endogenous variables between 0.848 and 0.912, all of them reached the limit (0.70) (Nunally, 1978; Churchill, 1979). Only the value of one variable – existential authenticity – proved to be just appropriate (0.70), however most of the values indicated strong consistency. Especially in case of low indicator numbers these results are preeminently favorable (Hair et al., 2009).

Based on the results of exploratory research, confirmative factor analysis was realized as the second step in order of a more rigorous investigation of the reliability and validity of the scales.

Analysis was realized by AMOS 20.0 software. The model fit in terms of **independent variables (service provider effect)** verified the factor number of 4 (previously revealed), in which the indicators of experience environment separated along two axles: (1) interactive experience environment and (2) operational experience environment. In Figure 12 the CFA measurement model of endogenous variables can be seen, whose model fits accomplished the adequacy criteria (see Table 11): CMIN/DF > 2 (Byrne, 1989), NFI > 0.9 (Bentler – Bonett, 1990), CFI > 0.9 (Bentler, 1999), RMSAE < 0.5 for close fit, < 0.8 for acceptable fit (Browne – Cudeck, 1993).

Table 11: CFA Model Fit

Model Fit	Service provider effect	Experience involvement	Experience outcome
CMIN/DF	2.401	2.920	3.034
NFI	.925	.902	.959
CFI	.955	.933	.972
RMSAE	.064	.074	.077
P	.000	.000	.000

Source: own construction

Figure 12: CFA – service provider effect

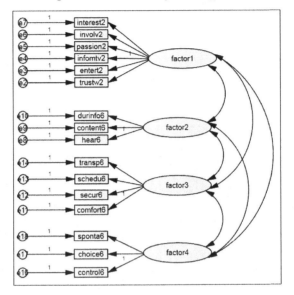

Source: AMOS 20.0, own construction (2013)

As the result of confirmative factor analysis, the **endogenous latent variables measuring experience** and their indicators altered to some degree compared to the exploratory factor analysis. In order to improve the model fit, the deletion of some indicators became justifiable based on the extreme values in the significance level and/or in the M.I. indicators (see Hair et al., 2009). The number of indicators of "flow-level involvement" factor decreased, while the factor of "general involvement" has separated into two: "emotional involvement" and "mental involvement", only the indicator structure of "social involvement" factor remained unchanged. CFA measurement model of endogenous variables can be seen in Figure 13, and Table 11 reviews the models fit values fulfilling the criteria.

Figure 13: CFA – experience involvement

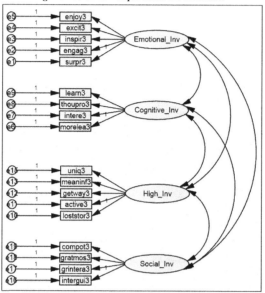

Source: AMOS 20.0, own construction (2013)

Based on the confirmative factor analysis, the modification of the experience-outcome: **endogenous variables measuring authenticity and memorability** was not needed – it had provided appropriate factor weights and model fit values in the revealed structure (see Table 11). Figure 14 reviews the factor structures.

Figure 14: CFA – experience outcome variables

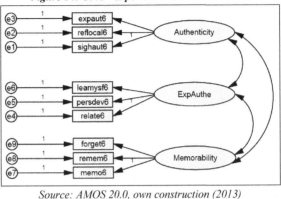

Source: AMOS 20.0, own construction (2013)

After having tested the measurement scales of latent variables, the relation among latent variables (see hypotheses) were investigated as the next step of the research.

9.3. Structural equation modeling

The quantitative research focuses on a measurement structure which forms a structural equation model. The structural equation modeling (SEM) is actually a method of scale validation, and testing the relations among certain variables (Gefen et al., 2000). We distinguish two types of structural equation modeling techniques: covariance based techniques (Amos, LISREL) and variance based techniques (e.g. Partial Least Squares - PLS). Structural equation models usually contain latent variables and indicators related to them, where the measurement model determines the orientation of the relations. These measurement models can be formative or reflective, due to the causal orientation of the relation between indicators and variables (see Henseler et al., 2009). It corresponds with Rossiter's (2002) proposal referring to the differentiation of the two scale types. Based on the conclusions of the previous scale development (see Chapter 7.3.), the structural model contains only reflective measurement models.

Implementation of covariance based SEM, such as Amos or LISREL was not justified because of two reasons. In one hand, the complexity of the measurement model was higher (13 latent variables) than it was recommended to measure in case of a 300-500 sample size (Hair et al., 2009). In other hand, covariance based SEM method is rather suitable to examine the goodness-of-fit of already existing models. In addition, it is rather used to refine the model, and it is used less typically to develop models or conceptions (Anderson – Gerbing, 1988; Henseler et al., 2009). Most of the authors suggest applying Partial Least Scale analysis (PLS) for exploratory model testing (Klarmann, 2011).

The variance based PLS path modeling method is similar to SEM is more suitable in many respects. It can be adapted to analyze complex models also in case of a relatively smaller sample size, too (Jöreskog, 1982). It means another advantage from the aspect of my research: it enables to analyze and compare the service provider types. Compared to SEM, PLS's disadvantage is that it cannot be applied for the measurement of goodness-of-fit of a given model (it measures R^2 only). Despite of this fact, it can be a more appropriate tool in the earlier stages of theory creation than SEM, as its predictive skills are better (Henseler et al., 2009). At the same time, PLS path modeling also stands for a reasonable methodological alternative for theory testing (Henseler et al., 2009).

As next step, the implement of PLS analysis took place with the help of SmartPLS 2.0 software. The model (Figure 15), constructed according to the scales resulting from the confirmative factor analysis, stands in the center of path analysis. Beside the path analysis the reliability and validity of the model was also analyzed with the software. Content validity, convergent validity and discriminant validity are three distinct types of validity. Content validity has already been discussed in details in a previous chapter. However convergent and discriminant validity can also be explored in case of the structural model. (Henseler et al., 2009).

Convergent validity explains to what extent a positive correlation exists between the scale and other indicators of the same concept (Malhotra, 2008). The application of so called average variance extracted (AVE) is suggested if the threshold of minimum 0,5 is an expectation, which indicates whether the latent variable is able to explain at least half of the indicator variances. In case of second order scales, consideration of other indicators is suggested because of its complexity (Rossiter, 2002). If the value of AVE has lower (but still higher than 0.4), but the indicator has an appropriate CR value (>0.8), the scale is valid (Ping, 2004).

During the **evaluation of reliability,** examination of *internal consistency* takes place. Cronbach-alpha is the indicator of internal consistency, which provides reliability estimation as the average of correlation coefficients resulted from the every possible dual division of scale items (Sajtos and Mitev, 2007). It represents into what extent are the statements of the scale consistent with the concept desired to be measured. The coefficient value usually increases with the number of scale items, so it's hard to result a higher Cronbach-alpha value if the scale has a lower number of items (Hair et al., 2009; Malhotra, 2002). However, in the present research even the scales with lower item number show appropriate values.

Beside Cronbach-alpha, the use of *CR (composite reliability)* indicator is also recommended, which takes into consideration not only the standardized factor weights, but the measurement error as well. Its threshold of acceptability is >0.7 (Hair et al., 2009; Henseler et al, 2009).

Crosstable is a widespread method of identifying **discriminant validity** on the basis of what the highest value of correlation among the latent variables can be 0.7. (Henseler et al., 2009). The discriminant validity of the model is appropriate.
Table 12 summarizes the main reliability and validity criteria of the model.

Table 12: Reliability and validity indicators of the model

Variables	AVE	CR	R^2	Cronbach-Alpha
Authenticity	0.5522	0.8783	0.4602	0.8303
Constructive authenticity	0.7677	0.9082	0.8296	0.8483
Customization	0.7408	0.8954		0.8238
Emotional experience-involvement	0.6505	0.9026	0.8267	0.8642
Existential authenticity	0.6378	0.8396	0.7412	0.717
Operational experience environment	0.6638	0.887		0.8293
Flow-like experience-involvement	0.6267	0.8933	0.8103	0.8505
Interaction	0.6812	0.9275		0.906
Experience involvement	0.4911	0.9452	0.6598	0.9382
Memorability	0.8242	0.9335	0.4574	0.8932
Mental experience-involvement	0.6839	0.8963	0.7575	0.8455
Social experience-involvement	0.7086	0.9065	0.5484	0.8616
Interactive experience environment	0.7222	0.8856		0.8077

Source: own construction (2013)

Reliability and validity criterions were evaluated also in case of the structural model. Consideration of the following indicators are recommended (Henseler et al, 2009):
- R^2 coefficient of determination (vide Chin, 1998) and
- the significance level of path-coefficients (t-values).

The **goodness-of-fit** of the structural model is confirmed by R^2 coefficient of determination referring to the endogenous latent variables, which on first level has resulted in **strong values** *(service provider effect -> experience (R^2 = 0.660)*, on second level in **medium values** *(service provider effect -> experience -> authenticity (R^2 = 0.46) and memorability (R^2 = 0.457))* (see Table 5). **This ensures an appropriate goodness-of-fit for the model, and demonstrates its operability. Based on the estimated values, it can be said that the exogenous variables account for the explained variance of experience involvement in 66%, of authenticity in 46% and of memorability in 45.7%.**

The value of path-coefficients are significant among some variables, but in case of some others they are not significant, hereby their role in the model has become doubtful. Coefficients will be discussed in more detail in the next subsection.

Figure 15: Path analysis

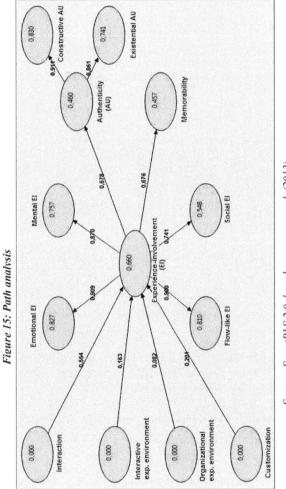

Source: SmartPLS 2.0, based on own research (2013)

The acceptance or the rejection of hypotheses of the structural model (Figure 16) can be determined based on the value of path-coefficients, namely the standardized regression coefficients (β), and their significance level can be assessed by bootstrapping procedure (>1.96).

Figure 16: Hypothesis model modified in consequence of CFA

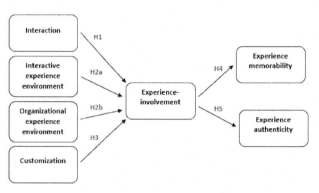

Source: own construction (2013)

H1: Interaction contributes to the degree of the consumer's experience involvement.

After examining the first hypothesis, we can state that there is a positive and significant correlation between the tour guidance **interaction** and experience-involvement ($\beta 1 = 0.5542$, $t=5.7476$). Hypothesis has been accepted.

H2: The experience environment contributes to the experience involvement.

Based on the factor analysis, experience environment separated to two parts, that's why the hypothesis has also been divided into two parts – H2a and H2b.

- **H2a: Interactive experience environment of the tour contributes to the involvement into a given experience.**

After analyzing the first part of the second hypothesis (H2a), we can state that there is a positive correlation between experience-involvement and the interactive experience environment, and this relation is evaluated to be significant based on t-test ($\beta 2_a = 0.1629$, t=2.0155). Hypothesis has been accepted.

- **H2b: Operational experience environment contributes to the involvement into a given experience.**

After analyzing the second part of the second hypothesis (H2b), it can be stated that there is a positive, however not significant correlation between the operational **experience environment** (provided by tour providers) and the experience-involvement ($\beta 2_b = 0.0817$, t=0.9279). So the hypothesis has been rejected.

H3: Perceived customization contributes to the involvement into a given experience.

Once analyzing the third hypothesis it became empirically proved that the customization of the tour and its flexibility have a positive and significant influence on experience- involvement ($\beta 3 = 0.2011$, t=3.401). Therefore the hypothesis has been accepted.

Based on the path-coefficient values (β) in terms of exogenous variables, it is found that tour guidance interaction (Interaction) is the factor, which influences experience-involvement (Experience) the most. Customization and flexibility of the tour (Customization) is the second most determinative factor.

H4: Experience involvement affects the perceived authenticity.

Related to the fourth hypothesis, results have confirmed that experience-involvement influences authenticity positively and significantly ($\beta 4 = 0.6784$, t=11.3747). So the hypothesis has been accepted.

H5: Experience involvement affects memorability.

Analysis of the fifth hypothesis has revealed that experience-involvement influences memorability positively and significantly ($\beta 4 = 0.6784$, t=11.3747). Therefore the hypothesis has been accepted.

The methodology enabled the implementation of PLS algorithm on the level of the **subsamples of the three service providers**, in order to reveal the differences and similarities among them. All in all it can be concluded that the structural model has resulted in similar outcomes in all three cases, which also overlaps with the whole model (see Appendix).

Reliability and validity indicators typically only varied slightly compared to the whole model. Goodness-of-fit indicators remained strong and moderate in all cases.

As a difference, it was revealed that the coefficient values of independent variables (Custom: $\beta_{Kis} = 0.3069$, Exp Envi: $\beta_{Kis} = 0.0542$, Interactiv: $\beta_{Kis} = 0.3334$, Tour Inte: 0.2689) were more balanced in case of *small-group tour providers*, while tour guiding interactivity seemed to influence experience-involvement to a bigger extent ($\beta_{Alte} = 0.6473$, $\beta_{Nagy} = 0.6113$, $\beta_{Kis} = 0.3334$) in case of the other two service providers.

After completing the bootstrapping procedure, latent variables with the lowest path-coefficients proved to be under the significance level. In case of *small-group tours*, the results showed similarity with the structural model of the whole sample, and only the operational experience environment variable had non-significant effect ($\beta = 0.0542$, $t = 0.5288$). In case of *big-group tours* neither the operational experience environment ($\beta = 0.099$, $t = 1.4027$) nor the interactive experience environment ($\beta = 0.0542$, $t = 1.8244$) proved to have significant effect. In case of *alternative tours*, operational experience-environment, interactive experience environment, and customization also showed positive but low path-coefficients ($\beta = 0.1576$, $t = 1.8221$), which did not prove to be significant.

Values of path-coefficients among endogenous latent variables examined in the structural model were similar in case of all the three subsample groups: between $0.6 - 0.7$, and significant.

Based on the examination of path-coefficients referring to each tour types, we can find that during *small-group tours* customization influencing experience-involvement almost to the same extent as the variable of interaction, and this is opposed to the two other tour types (alternative and big group tours) – where the latter has an outstanding influence (see Appendix).

Because the path-coefficients of tour types show different values, and the mean of their variables is various, there is no need for further t-test to prove the difference of the three subsamples.

The differences among tour types based on the means of examined variables is reviewed as next. Based on the results some conclusions are identified, as well.

In all cases **big group tours** received a lower evaluation (mean) of exogenous variables, than alternative and small group tours. The highest values were produced by small group tours. In case of the interaction, the interactive experience environment and the operational experience environment, the distribution of averages among tour types showed similar rates. The mean-value of interaction of big-group, bus tours fell one point behind the mean-value of small group, non-bus tours, while there was less than one tenth difference between live tour guidance and taped tour guidance. However, in case of customization, differences among the values showed a different structure.

Figure 17: The mean-values of service provider factors' variables

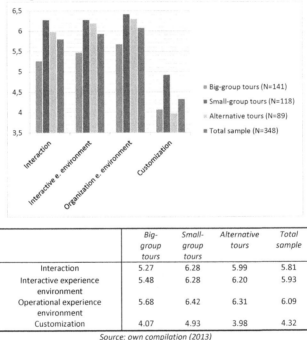

	Big-group tours	Small-group tours	Alternative tours	Total sample
Interaction	5.27	6.28	5.99	5.81
Interactive experience environment	5.48	6.28	6.20	5.93
Operational experience environment	5.68	6.42	6.31	6.09
Customization	4.07	4.93	3.98	4.32

Source: own compilation (2013)

Big-group tours did not reach high level of customization (4.07). If we look separately at HoHo tours belonging to this group, which presumably enabled a high degree of freedom for the guests, we can see that the value was higher only to a minor extent (4.34), and lagged behind the level of perceived customization of small-group tours (4.93). A conclusion can be made that despite the higher degree of freedom deriving from the service type, consumers do not perceive it that way. Its reason can be that the provider does not support the experience co-creation during the tour, and the consumer's experience involvement. It can be assumed that experience-centric management concept is able to support the perception of customization by applying methods of staged or co-created experience approaches. However, further research is needed in order to confirm this.

However **alternative tour providers** do apply experience management perspective, but it does not include the possibility of customization during the consumption (tour). Observations (without an exception) have revealed that alternative tour providers offered much less options to the participants during the tour. Their tours were less flexible, compared to other small group tours.

The influence of customization on experience-involvement was not at the same level in all cases, but where path-coefficients reached a higher value (in case of small group tours), an increased level of experience-involvement was achieved.

Figure 18: The mean-values of experience-involvement variables

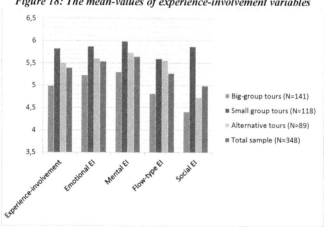

	Big-group tours	Small-group tours	Alternative tours	Total sample
Experience-involvement	4.99	5.83	5.51	5.39
Emotional EI	5.23	5.87	5.61	5.54
Mental EI	5.30	5.99	5.74	5.64
Flow-like EI	4.82	5.60	5.56	5.27
Social EI	4.41	5.87	4.73	4.99

Source: own construction (2013)

In case of the variables of experience-involvement it was observed that in all cases mental involvement was the most significant, although emotional involvement followed it with a small digression (around one tenth). Small-group tours reached the highest value and alternative tours took the second place.

If we examine the mean-value of experience-involvement along its dimensions, it can be observed that in case of alternative tours flow-like experience-involvement is represented with a higher average (compared to the other dimensions of the same tour type), than other tour types.

The other dimension worth mentioning is the social experience-involvement, which in case of small-group tours has reached outstanding averages compared to the other two types. This corresponds with the statements of qualitative research according to these tours are more interactive, and most of all they have a higher level of customization – so it is in accordance with this conclusion. In addition, if the type of the tour content is examined (and as other observations and interviews have already explored): alternative tours interpret serious issues of historical, social and other special themes, which probably effects the social interaction during the tour (as the observations show: there is less interaction within the group), which consequently can result in a lower degree of social experience-involvement.

Comparing the mean-values of endogenous outcome variables (Figure 19), it can be seen that memorability attained the highest value in case of small-group tours, while in case of alternative tours authenticity did it. In case of alternative tours, existential authenticity received a 0.5 higher mean compared to small-group tours, while mean-values of constructive authenticity were really close to each other, but still in favor of small-groups tours. Since the distribution rates were similar in case of flow-like and other experience-involvement dimensions, it can be assumed that correlation exists between flow-like experience-involvement and existential authenticity.

Big-group tours presented the lowest mean-values, however, in case of existential authenticity they underachieved in a great extent compared to the other two tour types. Likewise their mean-value of flow-like experience-involvement, which also lagged behind the other tour types. It raises further questions regarding to whether the influence is caused by the difference in group size, or in mean of transport, or another factor.

Figure 19: Mean-values of experience outcome factors' variables

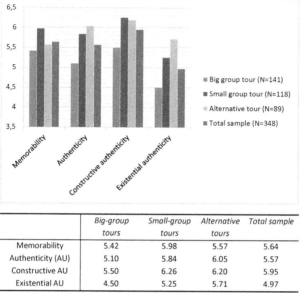

	Big-group tours	Small-group tours	Alternative tours	Total sample
Memorability	5.42	5.98	5.57	5.64
Authenticity (AU)	5.10	5.84	6.05	5.57
Constructive AU	5.50	6.26	6.20	5.95
Existential AU	4.50	5.25	5.71	4.97

Source: own construction (2013)

Furthermore, based on the results of the research it might be assumed that high level customization leads to higher memorability, as they appear to have a positive and direct relation.

Research did not aim to reach representativeness among service providers, so the results and conclusions within the tour types should not be generalized to all service providers. Instead, the research focused on the examination of casual relations in context of experience creation between the tourist and the tour provider.

One of the major results of the dissertation was brought by the research realized among tour providers, which was focusing at the investigation of the degree of experience-centric approach, and the observation of the modes of experience creation. As a qualitative research it resulted in an extent- and content rich data with explorative and descriptive profile.

Results explaining casual linkages, derived from quantitative research, aim to measure the linkages between service providers' impact on consumer experience, dimensions of consumer experience-involvement and its outcome factors, all of this in context of sightseeing tours.

Moreover, two other important results should be highlighted, which are determinative factors of the dissertation's theoretical, methodological, and practical relevance:

- the evolving of the Conceptual Frame of the Experience-centric Management approach, which is a result of literature review,
- the formation of the tourism experience-involvement scale, which was created by scale development procedure and structural equation modelling (SEM).

10.1. The Conceptual Frame of Experience-centric Management

The Conceptual Frame of Experience-centric Management was created based on literature review of experience economy and staged experiences (such as: Pine and Gilmore, 1998, 1999, Morgan, 2009, Lugosi, 2008), the concept of experience of co-creation (such as Prahalad and Ramaswamy, 2004, Payne et al., 2008, Binkhorst and Dekker, 2009, Prebensen and Foss, 2011). All of this was preceded by extended literature review between 2010 and spring of 2012 – before the research began. The Conceptual Frame (see Table 5) pointed out three frameworks or approaches: a general approach of experience-centric management and its framework, the framework of the staged experience concept, and the framework of experience co-creation concept.

- The experience-centric management approach puts consumer experience into the center of value creation process. That means that during service provision it privileges the experience of the consumer, and product development, organizational processes (e.g. knowledge-sharing) and other management aspects are adjusted according to it.

- Staged experience creation is a mode of experience-centric management, which views services and products as experiences, which are constructed, formed by the company, and offered to the customer consequently. To make the service truly experience-like and valuable for the customer, high-level organization and well written script is needed to produce a staged experience (drama).
- Experience co-creation is another mode of experience-centric management. The service provider view services as experience promises, from what the consumer produces the experience in collaboration with the service provider. The service provider can be viewed as experience-centric, if value creation process enables the involvement of the consumer to the experience. Meanwhile, the fact of co-creation also represents value for the customer.

The formation of the Conceptual Frame is the result of literature review, but based on the research results, often various experience creation approaches are used in practice. Only a small number of changes needed to be realized on the Conceptual Frame (mostly mergers of aspect items and changes in their order) – the frame proved to be a capable research tool.

10.2. The manifestation of experience-centric approach in practice

The qualitative results were complemented with the results of the quantitative research, which enabled to increase the validity of the quantitative, and the reliability of the qualitative research. The qualitative research lasted over a year, and produced a rich set of data on account of the 11 providers, 22 observed tours, 18 tour guide interviews, and 11 manager interviews included in the sample. Based on the type of the tour provider 3 subgroups were distinguished: small group, big group, and alternative tour providers.

Based on the conclusion and collation of the qualitative results it can be stated that the small group and alternative tours are characterized with the experience-centric perspective to the biggest extent. While in the area of management and operations of small group tour providers almost exclusively the approach of experience co-creation appears, but in case of alternative tour providers the approach of staged experience creation and experience co-creation are both applied. The management perspective of both types are experience-centric, however, some fields and management aspects are still seeking development in this direction.

Big group and bus type tour providers are characterized with the use of experience-centric approach in lower degree. The hindering facilities of acquiring experience-centric approach are arising from the specific features of the tour type (size of the group, the means of the transport causing passivity). However they try to manage these hindering facilities with an aim to provide a better experience, they perceive experience rather as a product supplementary. In their case there are more fields (in areas of product development and operations), which would need development to be more experience-centric. From the discussed approaches staged experience concept is the most typical in their case, which is mainly applied by one of the suppliers (RR). For HoHo type tour providers the concept of experience co-creation offers untapped opportunities and suitable methods of development.

The collation of the results enabled the evaluation of the assumptions of the qualitative study. Two assumptions were supported by the results of the study, according to what:

- Assumption 1: The experience-centric approach is mostly characteristic of small-scale tour providers.
- Assumption 2: In the case of alternative tour providers, the experience co-creation concept is the ruling principle.

One assumption got rejected by the results:

- Assumption 3: The staged experience concept is not predominant among any of the tour providers.

These results cannot be generalized internationally due to their place specific character. What can be deduced is that the means of the transport and the size of the group are two important factors, which can largely influence the use of the experience-centric approaches. As the research questions and results do not answer this, the investigation of such an assumption is suggested in the near future.

Based on quantitative research results the below conclusions were made concerning the hypotheses:

The hypotheses H1, H2a, H3, H4 and H5 received support from the empirical research, and they got accepted. It became empirically approved that:
- Interaction contributes to the degree of the consumer's involvement into a given experience.
- Interactive experience environment of the tour contributes to the involvement into a given experience.
- Perceived customization contributes to the involvement into a given experience.
- Experience involvement affects the memorability.
- Experience involvement affects the experience authenticity.

Hypothesis H2b got **rejected** based on the empirical results:
- Operational experience environment contributes to the involvement into a given experience.

Although the relation between organizational experience environment and experience-involvement proved to be positive, it does not reach the level of significance – so the effect of the independent variable is not significant. I would suggest the generalization of this result only in frames of this type of service (guided tour). Results of previous researches show that in case of different service types, variables such as satisfaction or quality are influenced by exogenous variables in different extent (see e.g. Rosen and Karwan, 1994, Crompton and Mackay, 1989). The major differences between service types depend on the degree of human interaction and staff intensity (Haywood-Farmer, 1988, Crompton and Mackay, 1989, Lovelock, 1984, Rosen and Karwan, 1994), the importance of physical environment and facility intensity (Lovelock, 1984, Frochot és Batat, 2013, Crompton and Mackay, 1989), degree of customization (Haywood-Farmer, 1988, Rosen and Karwan, 1994). Presumably, in case of a less interaction intensive service type the organizational experience environment has a bigger influence on consumer's experience-involvement. However, guided tours count to be a high staff intense, highly interactive, and high facility intense service type (Lovelock, 1984, Frochot and Batat, 2013, Crompton and Mackay, 1989), so it can be assumed that by the development of the environment and facilities used during service provision, the effect of the organizational environment factor will be increased.

By the comparison of the results of the qualitative and quantitative research the hypotheses H6 and H7 could be answered:

- H6: Tour providers preferring the experience-centric approach are able to reach a higher degree of involvement regarding the role of the tourist in experience-creation than providers preferring the non-experience-centric approach.
- H7: Tour providers mainly preferring the experience co-creation concept have the most success in involving the tourist into the process of experience-creation

Based on the results both hypothesis were accepted. Hypothesis H6 was supported, because the two tour provider types who proved to be experience-centric in their approach (the small group and alternative types), the mean-value of experience-involvement clearly higher (see Figure 12), than in case of big group tour providers, who do not apply an experience-centric approach (see Figure 19).

Hypothesis H7 got accepted, because small group tour providers have proved to apply the experience co-creation approach clearly to the biggest extent (see Figure 12), and they were the ones, who could involve the consumer to the experience the most (see Figure 19). The evaluation of hypotheses is concluded in Table 13.

Table 13: Evaluation of hypotheses

Hypothesis	Accepted	Based on
H1: Interaction contributes to the degree of the consumer's involvement into a given experience.	yes	PLS, path coefficient
H2a: The interactive content of the tour contributes to the involvement into a given experience.	yes	PLS, path coefficient
H2b: The organizational experience environment contributes to the involvement into a given experience.	no	PLS, path coefficient
H3: Perceived customization contributes to the involvement into a given experience.	yes	PLS, path coefficient
H4: Involvement into a given experience affects the memorability.	yes	PLS, path coefficient
H5: Involvement into a given experience affects the experience authenticity.	yes	PLS, path coefficient
H6: Tour providers preferring the experience-centric approach are able to reach a higher degree of involvement regarding the role of the tourist in experience-creation than providers preferring the non-experience-centric approach.	yes	PLS, path coefficient and qualitative result comparison
H7: Tour providers mainly preferring the experience co-creation concept have the most success in involving the tourist into the process of experience-creation.	yes	PLS, path coefficient and qualitative result comparison

Source: own compilation (2013)

The tourism experience involvement scale is also an important result of the thesis. The scale consisting of experience indicators based on literature review presents four dimensions of tourism experience involvement:

- emotional experience involvement,
- mental experience involvement,
- flow-like experience involvement,
- social experience involvement.

Emotional experience involvement results in an emotively perceived type of experience, such as: excitement, enjoyment, inspiration, fascination, surprise.

Mental experience involvement results in a cognitively perceived experience, such as: learning, activation of the desire to learn, something thought-provoking, interesting.

Flow-like experience involvement results in an emotive, yet cognitively perceived experience which is of conative and/or creative nature, and constitutes a higher level of involvement. The indicators measuring flow-like experience involvement examine the following factors: perception of uniqueness, meaningfulness, escapism, getting lost in the story created during the tour.

Social experience involvement refers to the social experience surfacing during the tour, which is determined by the interactions of the participants. This is an essential dimension of each and every experience that is created with the participation of a group of individuals. The indicators measuring the level of social involvement are: group atmosphere, enjoying the company of fellow group members, the amount of interaction within the group, and the amount of interaction with the frontline employee (guide).

11. CONCLUSION

11.1. Academic significance

The results of the thesis are well-suited for the current development of tourism literature. When choosing the topic of the thesis, one of the most influential deciding factors was to come up with something that is both closely connected to international research trends and can be regarded as a currently relevant problem from a professional point of view. The chosen topic set out to fill a void in literature by examining the tourism experience from the supplier's side. Consequently, the thesis has the potential to gain international significance.

The academic significance of the thesis lies in the empirical examination of the dimensions of the experience, in scheming up the conceptual boundaries of the experience-centric management, and, last not least, in examining the tourism experience from the supplier's side with qualitative and quantitative empiricism.

Furthermore, the empirical research produced explorative results – a prime example being the various manifestations of the concepts of the experience-centric approach, which, if supplemented with relevant researches – thus increasing their reliability -, can contribute to the field's ever-growing basis of knowledge.

The hypotheses originating from the theory empirically tested the coherences, and the majority of them were proven to be true – further increasing their scientific significance. The coherencies proven to be false by the research also led to useful conclusions, although their thorough rejection requires further research.

The structural model schemed up in the research was deemed partially acceptable, and the results of the research, hand in hand with a research questioning the theory, can give life to new discussions within academic circles. Moreover, the miscellaneous factors that surfaced while scheming up the structural model might inspire further researches and tests, which are introduced in the chapter discussing the future research options.

11.2. Methodological significance

Based on the results it can be suggested that on account of scale development procedures already in the present stage, results are characterized with explanatory value, and structural model of supplier-side experience creation in aspect of all endogenous variables, and except of one, all exogenous variables testified an acceptable goodness-of-fit.

The mixed methodology can be viewed as one of the methodological importance of the doctoral dissertation. It aimed and enabled to analyze the researched topic in-depth and multilayered form. In the area of scientific researches about the current topic there are only few published researches with mixed methodology.

Application of SEM (structural equation modeling) method into the investigation of tourism experience and experience creation can be perceived as another methodological significance. During literature review I did not find any publication, which would apply PLS (Partial Least Square). However, several questions are waiting to be answered, and where PLS could be a right tool to use. Therefore, the thesis and current research might have an impact of spreading this technique among the academic researchers of the topic.

11.3. Practical significance

Since data collection was carried out directly on the field in cooperation with tourism service providers, the practical relevance of the results is overwhelming, thus the conclusions can be put into practice.

The practical significance of the thesis reaches far beyond the boundaries of tour guides and tour providers, and extends to and perhaps beyond the entirety of tourism and leisure. The results (which, first and foremost, cover the tools and methods of experience creation) can be applied by and useful for those professional fields, providers, and companies that intend to put the experience-centric approach into practice in their strategies or work processes.

During certain phases of the research, reliability and validity considerations, and also testing methods of these criteria were described in details. All along the research process reliability and validity were deliberated.

The sampling, instead of being representative from the perspective of the composition of Budapest's tourists, it applied a random sampling methodology from the perspective of the service providers. The tour observation were chosen randomly to the sample, and at the end of the tour, all the participated customers were offered the possibility to fill in the questionnaire. An acceptable sample size was reached both from service provider's, both from customer's side.

The primary aim of the research is reflected in exploration of interrelations, which was enabled by investigating tourist experience creation from a multifaceted and complex process view (from perspective of stakeholders: management, guide, and tourist).

To what extent can be the result applied in other fields? The application of experience-centric approach is suitable in other sectors, too, not only tourism. The presentation of results (especially from the observation) practical methods of experience creation are found and collected. It is suggested that these result are applicable also in the marketing and management of other fields.

11.5. Limitations

During the analyzes of the results it has appeared that compared to more complex algorithmic models, the sample size of the research was not enough – so covariance based SEM analyzes with AMOS software (which analyzes multiply goodness-of-fit indicators at the same time) could not be realized.

Organized leisure and incentive groups were included to the sample originally, but during the data collection I faced limitations resulting in a decision to exclude these tour types from the sample. In case of or organized leisure groups the multi-stakeholder tour organizing made impossible the data collection (permissions from all, 3 or more organizational stakeholders of the tour, which despite of several trials, could not be reached).

In case of incentive tours, shortly after the observation has started, I could experience their highly customized nature, so the result would not be suitable for generalizability. The closed character of the groups, which did not allow to observe every moment of the tour (e.g. interactive games). The lack of the possibility of relevant data collecting after three observed tours, lead to a decision to shut down this branch of the studied tour types.

Another limitation was that some tour providers (Eurama, Imagine Budapest, Unique Budapest) wanted to participate only in the qualitative part of the research.

Furthermore, related to methodological considerations I refer several times to financial and time resource shortage, which also delimits the application of bigger sample size. Presentation and analyzes of the further research results were not possible because of the length limits of the thesis.

11.6. Future research

As first of recommendations for future research I would highlight further testing of the structural model. The model needs further clarification to become a methodologically well-defined construct. For this purpose (except of the already realized PLS analyzes) testing with Amos or LISREL software would be needed to assure a rigorous goodness-of-fit for the model.

Studying the experience-involvement in various fields and sectors could bring interesting results about the stability and variability of the dimensions of the experience-involvement construct.

Although blog analysis (netnography) was performed with a complementary purpose, and was included to the research as part of the scale development, in the field of tourism it can be viewed as an effective, and from methodological perspective advantageous data source, which demand more attention from the researchers of the field.

I would suggest to realize the research on the international scene, too, because as for now its qualitative part has been realized only among Hungarian tour and program providers in Budapest. It would be useful to investigate that in other destinations to what extent is experience-centric approach popular as a management and marketing concept, and what kind of methods are in use.

12. REFERENCE LIST

Addis, M. – Holbrook, M. B. (2001). On the conceptual link between mass customization and experiential consumption: An explosion of subjectivity. Journal of Consumer Behaviour, Vol. 1, No. 1, pp. 50-66.

Aho, S. K. (2001). Towards a general theory of touristic experiences: modeling experience process in Tourism, Tourism Review, Vol. 56, No. 3-4, pp. 33–37.

Amis, J. – Silk, M. L. (2010). Transnational Organization and Symbolic Production: Creating and Managing a Global Brand, Consumption Markets and Culture, Vol. 13, No. 2, pp. 159-179.

Andereck, K. – Bricker, K. S. – Kerstetter, D. – Nickerson, N. P. (2006). Connecting experiences to quality: Understanding the meanings behind visitors' experiences. In G. Jennings – N. P. Nickerson (eds.) Quality Tourism Experiences, Elsevier Butterworth-Heinemann, Burlington, MA, pp. 81-98.

Andersson, T. D. (2007). The tourist in the experience economy, Scandinavian Journal of Hospitality and Tourism, Vol. 7, No. 1, pp. 46-58.

Arnould, E. J. – Price, L. (2000). Authenticating Acts and Authoritative Performances: Questing for Self and Community. In S. Ratneshwar – D. G. Mick – C. Huffman (eds.) The Why of Consumption: Contemporary Perspectives on Consumer Motives, Goals and Desires, Routledge, New York, pp. 140-163.

Arsenault, N. – Gale, T. (2004). Defining Tomorrow's Tourism Product: Packaging Experiences, Canadian Tourism Commission. Research Report 2004-7.

Babbie, E. (2001). A társadalomtudományi kutatás gyakorlata [The practice of social research], Balassi Kiadó, Budapest.

Belk, R. W. (1975). Situational variables and consumer behavior, Journal of Consumer Research, Vol. 2, No. 3, pp. 157-164.

Berry, L. – Zeithaml, V. – Parasuraman, A. (1985). Quality counts in services too, Business Horizons, Vol. 28, pp. 44-52.

Binkhorst E. – Dekker T. Den (2009). Agenda for Co-Creation Tourism Experience Research, Journal of Hospitality Marketing & Management, Vol. 18, No. 2, pp. 311-327.

Bitner, M. J. (1992). Servicescapes: the Impact of physical surroundings on customers and employees, Journal of Marketing, Vol. 56, No. 2, pp. 57-71.

Boorstin, D. (1964). The Image: A guide to pseudo-events in America, Harper, New York.

Borrie, W. – Roggenbuck, J. W. (2001). The dynamic, emergent, and multi-phasic nature of on-site wilderness experiences, Journal of Leisure Research, Vol. 33, No. 2, pp. 202-228.

Boswijk, A. – Thijssen, T. – Peelen, E. (2005). Een nieuwe kijk op de experience economy, betekenisvolle belevenissen, Pearson Education Benelux, Amsterdam.

Boswijk, A. – Thijssen, T. – Peelen, E. (2007). The experience economy, a new perspective. Pearson Education Benelux, Amsterdam.

Botterill, D. T. – Crompton, J. L. (1996). Two case studies exploring the nature of the tourist's experience. Journal of Leisure Research, Vol. 28, No. 1, pp. 57-82.

Braun-LaTour, K. A. – LaTour, M. S. (2005). Transforming consumer experience when timing matters, Journal of Advertising, Vol. 34, No. 3, pp. 19–30.

Buhalis D. (2003). eTourism: Information Technology for Strategic Tourism Management, FT Prentice Hall, London.

Carlson, R. (1997). Experienced Cognition. Lawrence Erlbaum Association, New York.

Caru, A. – Cova, B. (2003). Revisiting consumption experience: A more humble but complete view of the concept, Marketing Theory, Vol. 3, No. 2, pp. 267-286.

Caru, A. – Cova, B. (2007). Consumption Experience, Routledge, London.

Cary, S. H. (2004). The tourist moment, Annals of Tourism Research, Vol. 31, No. 1, pp. 61–77.

Chhetri, P. – Arrowsmith, C. – Jackson, M. (2004). Determining hiking experiences in nature-based tourist Destinations, Tourism Management, Vol. 25, No. 1, pp. 31–43.

Chikán, A. (2003). Vállalatgazdaságtan [Business Economics], Aula Kiadó, Budapest, pp. 92-116.

Churchill, G. A. (1995). Marketing Research: Methodological Foundations, Dryden Press, Fort Worth, Texas.

Clawson, M. (1963). Land and water for recreation: opportunities, policies and problems, Rand McNally, New York.

Clawson, M. – Knetsch, J. (1966). Economics of Outdoor Recreation, John Hopkins, Baltimore.

Cohen, E. (1972). Towards a sociology of international tourism, Social Research, Vol. 39, pp. 164–189.

Cohen, E. (1979). A Phenomenology of Tourism Experiences, Sociology, Vol. 13, pp. 179–201.

Cole ,S. T. – Scott, D. (2004). Examining the mediating role of experience quality in a model of tourists experiences, Journal of Travel and Tourism Marketing, Vol. 16, No. 1, pp. 77–88.

Cova, B. – Cova, V. (2002). Tribal Marketing: The Tribalisation of Society and Its Impact on the Conduct of Marketing, European Journal of Marketing, Vol. 36, No. 5, pp. 595–620.

Cova, B. – Dalli, D. (2009). Working consumers: the next step in marketing theory? Marketing Theory, Vol. 9, No. 3, pp. 315-339.

Cova, B. – Pace, S. (2006). Brand Community of Convenience Products: New Forms of Customer Empowerment – the Case "My Nutella the Community", European Journal of Marketing 40, No. 9/10, pp. 1087–1105.

Crawford, J. – Kippax, S. – Onyx, J. – Gault, U. – Benton, P. (1992). Emotion and Gender: Constructing Meaning from Memory. Stage, London.

Cronin, J. J. – Taylor, S. A. (1992). Measuring Service Quality: A re-examination and extension, Journal of Marketing, Vol. 56, pp. 66-68.

Crompton, J. L. – Mackay, K. J. (1989). User's perceptions of the relative importance of service quality dimensions in selected public recreation programs, Leisure Sciences, Vol. 11, pp. 367-375.

Csikszentmihalyi, M. (1975). Beyond Boredom and Anxiety: The Experience of Play in Work and Games, Jossey-Bass Publishers, San Francisco.

Csikszentmihalyi, M. (1990). Flow: The Psychology of Optimal Experience – Steps Toward Enhancing the Quality of Life, HarperCollins Publisher, New York.

Cutler, S. Q. – Carmichael, B. A. (2010). The Dimension of the Tourist Experience. In M. Morgan– P. Lugosi – J.R.B. Ritchie (eds.) The Tourism and Leisure Experience: Consumer and Managerial Perspectives, Channel View Publications, Bristol, pp. 3-26.

Davenport, T. H. – Beck, J. C. (2001). The Attention Economy, Harvard Business School Press, New York.

Dolcos, F. – Cabeza, R. (2002). Event-Related Potentials of Emotional Memory: Encoding Pleasant, Unpleasant, and Neutral Pictures, Cognitive, Affective & Behavioral Neuroscience, Vol. 2, No. 3, pp. 252–263.

Eco, U. (1986). Travels in hyper reality: Essays, Harcourt Brace Jovanovich, San Diego.

ETC (2006). Tourism Trends for Europe. European Travel Commission, Brussels, http://www.etc-corporate.org/resources/uploads/ETC_Tourism_Trends_for_Europe_09-2006_ENG.pdf, (downloaded 18/09/2011)

Etgar, M. (2008). A Descriptive Model of the Consumer Co-production Process, Journal of the Academy of Marketing Science, Vol. 36, No. 1, pp. 97–108.

Euro RSCG Worldwide Knowledge Exchange (2010). The future of travel: The New Vocabulary of Travel and Tourism, Know, Vol. 7, August, +http://www.thenewconsumer.com/2010/08/01/the-new-vocabulary-of-travel-and-tourism/#more-444 (downloaded: 16/12/2011).

Feifer, M. (1985). Going Places: The ways of the tourist from imperial Rome to the present day, Macmillan, London.

Filser, M. (2002). Le marketing de production d'expreinces: Statut théorique et implications managériales [Marketing production expreinces: status of theoretical and managerial implications], Désicions Marketing, Vol. 28, No. 4, pp. 13-22.

Firat, A.F. – Dholakia, N. (2006). Theoretical and Philosophical Implications of Postmodern Debates: Some Challenges to Modern Marketing, Marketing Theory, Vol. 6, No. 2, pp. 123–162.

Firat, A.F. – Dholakia, N. – Venkatesh, A. (1995). Marketing in a Postmodern World, European Journal of Marketing, Vol. 29, No. 1, pp. 40–56.

Firat, A. F. – Venkatesh, A. (1995). Liberatory Postmodernism and the Reenchantment of Consumption, Journal of Consumer Research, Vol. 22, No. 3, pp. 239-267.

Fisher, D. – Smith, S. (2011). Cocreation is chaotic: What it means for marketing when no one has control, Marketing Theory, Vol. 11, No. 3, pp. 325-350.

Florida, R. (2002). The rise of the creative class, Basic Books, New York.

Foster, R. J. (2011). The Uses of Use Value: Marketing, Value Creation, and the Exigencies of Consumption Work, In D. Zwick – J. Cayla (eds.) Inside Marketing, Practices, Ideologies, Devices, Oxford University Press: Oxford and New York, pp. 42-57.

Fredrickson, B. L. (2000). Extracting meaning from past affective experiences: The importance of peaks, ends and specific emotions, Cognition and Emotion, Vol. 14, pp. 577–606.

Frochot, I. – Batat, W. (2013). Markering and Designing the Tourist Experience. Goodfellow Publisher, London.

Gabriel, Y. – Lang, T. (2008). New Faces and New Masks of Today's Consumer, Journal of Consumer Culture, Vol. 8, No. 3, pp. 321–340.

Gentile, C. – Spiller, N. – Noci, G. (2007). How to Sustain the Customer Experience: An Overview of Experience Components that Co-create Value with the Consumer, European Management Journal, Vol. 25, No. 5, pp. 395-410.

Ghauri, P. – Gronhaug, K. (2011). Kutatásmódszertan az üzleti tudományokban, Akadémiai Kiadó, Budapest.

Gibbs, D. – Ritchie, C. (2010). Theatre in Restaurants: Constructing the Experience, 182-201. In Morgan M., Lugosi P., Ritchie J. R. B. (eds.) The Tourism and Leisure Experience: Consumer and Managerial Perspectives. Channel View Publications: Bristol.

Gillespie, C. (2001). European Gastronomy into the 21st Century. Elsevier Butterworth Heinemann, Oxford.

Gilmore H. J., Pine II B. J. (2002a) The Experience IS the Marketing. Amazon.com eDoc: Brown Herron Publishing.

Gilmore H. J., Pine II B. J. (2002b) Differentiating Hospitality Operations Via Experiences: Why Selling Services is Not Enough, Cornell Hotel and Restaurant Administration Quarterly, Vol. 43, No. 3, pp. 87–96.

Go, F. M. (2005). Co-creative tourists: An idea whose time has come. In P. Keller – T. Bieger (eds.), AIEST 55th Congress: Innovation in Tourism – Creating customer value, Assiciation Internationale d'Experts Scientifique du Tourisme, St. Gallen, Switzerlan, Vol. 47, pp. 77-89.

Gobe, M. – Gob, M. – Zyman, S. (2001). Emotional branding: The new Paradigm for connecting brands to people, Allworth Press, New York.

Goffman, E. (1959). The presentation of self in everyday life, Doubleday, New York.

Graefe, A. R. – Vaske, J. J. (1987). A framework for managing quality in the tourist experience. Annals of Tourism Research, Vol. 14, pp. 390–404.

Gronroos, C. (1985). Internal marketing – theory and practice. In T. Bloch – G. Upah – V. Zeithaml (eds.) Services Marketing in a Changing Environment, American Marketing Association, Chicago, pp. 41-47.

Gronroos, C. (2008). Service Logic Revisited: Who Creates Value? And Who Co-Creates?, European Business Review, Vol. 20, No.4, pp. 298–314.

Gross, M. J. – Brown, G. (2006). Tourism experiences in a lifestyle destination setting: The roles of involvement and place attachment, Journal of Business Research, Vol. 59, pp. 696-700.

Grove, S. J. – Fisk, R. P. (1989). Impression management in service experience: A managerial approach. In T. A. Swartz – S. Brown – D. Bowen (eds.) Advances in Service Marketing and Management, CT: JAI Press, Greenwich, pp. 427-438.

Grove, S. J. – Fisk, R. P. – Bitner, M. J. (1992). Dramatising the service experience: A managerial approach. In T. A. Swartz – S. Brown – D. Bowen (eds.) Advances in Service Marketing and Management, CT: JAI Press, Greenwich, pp. 91-121.

Haywood-Farmer, J. (1988). A conceptual model of service quality, International Journal of Operations and Productions Management, Vol. 8, No. 6, pp. 19-29.

Holbrook, M. B. – Hirschman, E. C. (1982). The experiential aspects of consumption: consumer fantasies, feelings, and fun, Journal of Consumer Research, Vol. 9, September, pp. 132–140.

Holbrook, M. B. (2001). Times Square, Disneyphobia, HegeMickey, the Ricky Principle, and the downside of the entertainment economy, Marketing Theory, Vol. 1, No. 2, pp. 139–163.

Holbrook, M. B. (2006). Consumption Experience, Customer Value, and Subjective Personal Introspection: An Illustrative Photographic Essay, Journal of Business Research, Vol. 59, No. 6, pp. 714–725.

Holt, D. B. (1995). How Consumers Consume – a Typology of Consumption Practices, Journal of Consumer Research, Vol. 22, No. 1, pp. 1-16.

Holyfield, L. (1999). Manufacturing adventure: The Buying and Selling of Emotions, Journal of Contemporary Ethnography, Vol. 28, February, pp. 3-32.

Hosany, S. – Gilbert, D. (2009). Measuring Tourists's Emotional Experiences toward Hedonic Holiday Destinations, Journal of Travel Research, Vol. 49, No. 4, pp. 513-526.

Hulten, B. – Broweus, N. – Van Dijk, M. (2009). Sensory Marketing, Palgrave Macmillan, London.

Jager, A. K. de (2009). The new tourist and co-creation as a key element of tourism destinations' competitiveness. In New challenges in the tourism and hospitality industry: dedicated to the 40th anniversary of higher education in Hungarian tourism and the Hotel Association of Hungary, Budapest Business School, Budapest, pp. 115-122.

Jaworski, B. – Kohli, A.K. (1993). Market Orientation: Antecedents and Consequences, Journal of Marketing, Vol. 57, No. 3, pp. 53–70.

Jennings, G. – Lee, Y. S. – Ayling, A. – Lunny, B. – Cater, C. – Ollenburg, C. (2009) Quality Tourism Experiences: Reviews, Reflections, Research agendas, Journal of Hospitality Marketing and Management, Vol. 18, No. 2, pp. 294-310.

Kim, J. H. – Ritchie, J. R. B. – McCormick, B. (2010). Development of a Scale to Measure Memorable Tourism Experiences, Journal of Travel Research, Vol. 20, No. 10, pp. 1–14.

King, J. (2002). Destination marketing organizations — connecting the experience rather than promoting the place, Journal of Vacation Marketing, Vol. 8, No. 2, pp. 105–108.

Kotler, P. – Adam, S. – Brown, L. – Armstrong, G. (2001). Principles of Marketing, Pearson – Prentice Hall, Frenchs Forest, Australia.

Krippendorf, J. (1986). Tourism in the System of Industrial Society, Annals of Tourism Research, Vol. 13, No. 4, pp. 393-414.

Kvale, S. (1996). Interviews: An Introduction to Qualitative Research Interviewing, Sage, Thousand Oaks, CA.

Ladwein, R. (2002). Voyage á Tikidad: de 1 'accés á l'expérience de consummation [Travelling to Tikidad: the access of consumption experiences], Décision Marketing, Vol. 28, No. 4, pp. 53-63.

Lashley, C. (2008). Marketing hospitality and tourism experiences. In H. Oh – A. Pizam (eds.), Handbook of Hospitality Marketing Management. Butterwood-Heinemann, Oxford, UK, pp. 552.

Larsen, S. (2007). Aspects of a Psychology of the Tourist Experience, Scandinavian Journal of Hospitality and Tourism, Vol. 7, No. 1, pp. 7-18.

LaSalle, D. – Britton, T. A. (2003). Priceless: Turning ordinary products into extraordinary experiences, Harvard Business School Press, Boston.

Lash, S. – Urry, J. (1994). Economies of Signs and Spaces, Sage, London.

Lawrence, T.B. – Phillips, N. (2002). Understanding Cultural Industries, Journal of Management Inquiry, Vol. 11, No. 4, pp. 430–441.

Lewis, R. C. – Chambers, R. E. (2000). Marketing Leadership in Hospitality, John Wiley, New York.

Li, X. – Petrick, J. F. (2008). Tourism Marketing in an Era of Paradigm Shift, Journal of Travel Research, Vol. 46, pp. 235-244.

Li, Y. (2000). Geographical consciousness and tourism experiences, Annals of Tourism Research, Vol. 27, No. 4, pp. 863-883.

Lichrou, M. – O'Malley, L. – Patterson, M. (2008). Place-product or place narrative(s)? Perspectives in the Marketing of the Tourism Destinations, Journal of Strategic Marketing, Vol. 16, No. 1, pp. 27-39.

Lofland, J. – Lofland, L. H. (1995). Analyzing Social Settings: A Guide to Qualitative Observation and Analysis, Wadsworth, Belmont, CA.

Lovelock, C.H. (1984). Services Marketing. Englewood Cliffs, Prentice Hall, New York.

Lugosi, P. (2007). Consumer participation in commercial hospitality, International Journal of Culture, Tourism and Hospitality Research, Vol. 1, No. 3, pp. 227-236.

Lusch, R. F. – Vargo, S. L. – O'Brien, M. (2006). Competing through Service: Insights from Service-dominant Logic, Journal of Retailing, Vol. 83, No. 1, pp. 5-18.

MacCannell, D. (1973). Staged authenticity: arrangements of social space in tourist settings, American Journal of Sociology, Vol. 79, No. 3, pp. 589-603.

MacCannell, D. (1976). The Tourist: A New Theory of the Leisure Class, Schocken, New York.

Malhotra, N. K. – Simon, J. (2009). Marketingkutatás [Marketing Research], Akadémia Kiadó, Budapest.

Mannell, R.C. – Iso-Ahola, S.E. (1987). Psychological nature of leisure and tourism experience, Annals of Tourism Research, Vol. 14, pp. 314–331.

Masberg, B. A. – Silverman, L. H. (1996). Visitor experiences at heritage sites, Journal of Travel Research, Vol. 34, No. 4, pp. 20-31.

Maslow, A. H. (1970). Motivation and Personality, Harper and Row Publisher Inc., New York.

McIntosh, A.J. – Siggs, A. (2005). An exploration of the experiential nature of boutique accommodation, Journal of Travel Research, Vol. 44, No. 1, pp. 74–81.

Mehmetoglu, M. – Engen, M. (2011). Pine and Gilmore's Concept of Experience Economy and Its Dimensions: An Empirical Examination in Tourism, Journal of Quality Assurance in Hospitality and Tourism, Vol. 12, pp. 237-255.

Meuter, M. L. – Ostrom, A. L. – Roundtree, R. I. – Bitner, M. J. (2000). Self-service technologies: understanding customer satisfaction with technology-based service encounters. Journal of Marketing, Vol. 64, pp. 50-64.

Michalkó, G. – Rátz, T. (2005). A kulturális turizmus élmény-gazdaságtani szempontjai [The experience economy aspects of cultural tourism]. In Gy. Egyedi – K. Keresztély (2005), A magyar városok kulturális gazdasága [Cultural economy of Hungarian cities], MTA Társadalomkutató Központ, Budapest, pp. 123-141.

Milligan, A. – Smith, S. (2002). Uncommon Practice: People Who Deliver a Great Brand Experience Harlow, Ft Prentice Hall, London.

Morgan, M. (2010). The Experience Economy 10 Years On: Where Next for Experience Management. In M. Morgan– P. Lugosi – J.R.B. Ritchie (eds.) The Tourism and Leisure Experience: Consumer and Managerial Perspectives, Channel View Publications, Bristol, pp. 218-230.

Morgan, M. – Elbe, J. – Curiel de Esteban, J. (2009). Has the experience economy arrived? The views of destination managers in three visitor-dependent areas, International Journal of Tourism Research, Vol. 11, pp. 201–216.

Morgan, N. – Pritchard, A. (2005). On souvenirs and metonymy: Narratives of memory, metaphor and materiality. Tourist Studies, Vol. 5, No. 1, pp. 29-53.

Mossberg, L. (2007). A marketing approach to the tourist experience. Scandinavian Journal of Hospitality and Tourism, Vol. 7, No. 1, pp. 59-74.

Moutinho, L. (1987). Consumer Behavior in Tourism, MCB University Press, New York.

Nickerson, N. P. (2006). Some reflections on quality tourism experiences. In G. Jennings – N. P. Nickerson (eds.) Quality Tourism Experiences, MA: Elsevier Butterworth-Heinemann, Burlington, pp. 227-236.

Nijs, D. (2003). Imagineering: engineering for imagination in the emotion economy. In F. Peeters – F. Schouten – D. Nijs (eds.) Creating a Fascinating World, NHTV, Breda, pp. 15–32.

O'Dell, T. (2005). Experiencescapes: Blurring Borders and Testing Connections. In T. O'Dell – P. Billing (eds.) Experiencescapes: Tourism, Culture and Economy. Copenhagen Business School Press, Copenhagen, pp. 11-33.

O'Sullivan, E. L. – Spangler, K. J. (1998). Experience Marketing – Startegies for the New Millenium. Venture Publishing, Inc. State College.

Onyx, J. – Small, J. (2001). Memory-work: The method, Qualitative Inquiry, Vol. 7, No. 6, pp. 773-786.

Ooi, C. (2005). Theory of Tourism Experiences: The Management of Attention. In T. O'Dell – P. Billing (eds.) Experiencescapes: Tourism, Culture, and Economy. Copenhagen Business School Press, Copenhagen, pp. 11-33.

Page, S. J. – Brunt, P. – Busby, G. – Connell, J. (2001). Tourism: A modern synthesis, Thomson Learning, London.

Payne, A. – Storbacka, K. – Frow, P. (2008). Managing the co-creation of value, Journal of the Academical Marketing Science, Vol. 36, pp. 83–96.

Pearce, P. (1982). The Social Psychology of Tourist Behavior, International Series in Experiential Psychology, Vol. 3, Pergamon, Oxford.

Petkus, E. (2004). Enhancing the application of experiential marketing in the arts, International Journal of Nonprofit and Voluntary Sector Marketing, Vol. 9, No. 1, pp. 49–57.

Pine, B. J. – Gilmore, J. H. (1998). Welcome to the experience economy: Work is theatre and every business is a stage, Harvard Business Review, Vol. 76, No. 4, pp. 97-105.

Pine, B. J. – Gilmore, J. H. (1999). The Experience Economy: Work is Theatre & Every Business a Stage, Harvard Business School Press, Boston.

Poon, A. (1993). Tourism, Technology and Competitive Strategies, CAB, Wallingford.

Prahalad, C. K. (2004). Co-creation of Value, Invited Commentaries on "Evolving to a New Dominant Logic for Marketing", Journal of Marketing, Vol. 68, January, pp. 18-27.

Prahalad, C. K. – Ramaswamy, V. (2000). Co-opting Customer Competence, Harvard Business Review, Vol. 78, January, pp. 79-90.

Prahalad, C. K. – Ramaswamy, V. (2003). The New Frontier of Experience Innovation, Sloan Management Review, Vol. 44, Summer, pp. 12-18.

Prahalad, C. K. – Ramaswamy, V. (2004a). The Future of Competition: Co-creating Unique Value with Customers, Harvard Business School Press, Boston.

Prahalad, C. K. – Ramaswamy, V. (2004b). Co-creation Experiences: The Next Practice in Value Co-creation. Journal of Interactive Marketing, Vol. 18, No. 3, pp. 5-14.

Prebensen, N. K. – Foss, L. (2011). Coping and co-creating in tourist experiences, *International Journal of Tourism Research*, Vol. **13,** No. 1, pp. 54-67.

Puczkó, L. (2009). A szabad munkától a munkás szabadságig – és vissza! [From free-time work to working holiday – and back!], Magyar Fogyasztó [The Hungarian Consumer], No. 1, pp 24-26. http://www.magyarfogyaszto.hu/file/MFSZ_SZI.pdf (downloaded: 15/02/2012).

Puczkó, L. – Rátz, T. (2011). Az attrakciótól az élményig: A látogatómenedzsment módszerei [From Attractions to Experiences: Methods of Visitor Management], Geomédia Kiadó, Budapest.

Quan, S. – Wang, N. (2004). Towards a structural model of the tourist experience: An illustration from food experiences in tourism, Tourism Management, Vol. 25, pp. 297–305.

Ray, A. (2008). Experiential Art: Marketing Imitating Art Imitating Life, elérhetőség: http://www.experiencetheblog.com/2008/05/experiential-art-marketing-imitating.html, (downloaded: 20/03/2011).

Richards, G. – Wilson, J. (2006). Developing creativity in tourist experiences: A solution to the serial reproduction of culture? Tourism Management, Vol. 27, pp. 1209–1223.

Ritchie, J. R. B. – Hudson, S. (2009). Understanding and Meeting the Challenges of Consumer/Tourist Experience Research, International Journal of Tourism Research, Vol. 11, pp. 111–126.

Ritchie, J. R. B. – Tung, V. W. S. – Ritchie, R. J. B. (2011). Tourism Experience Management Research: Emergence, Evolution and Future Directions, International Journal of Contemporary Hospitality Management, Vol. 23, No. 4, pp. 419-438.

Ritzer, G. – Liska, A. (1997). McDisneyization and post-tourism: Complementary perspectives on contemporary tourism. In C. Rojek – J. Urry (eds.) Touring Cultures: Transformation of Travel and Theory, Routledge, London, pp. 96-109.

Ritzer, G. – Jurgenson, N. (2010). Production, Consumption, Prosumption: The nature of capitalism in the age of the digital "prosumer", Journal of Consumer Culture, Vol. 10, No. 1, pp. 13-36.

Rojek, C. (1993). Disney culture, Leisure Studies, Vol. 12, No. 2, pp. 121-135.

Rosen, L.D. – Karwan, K.R. (1994). Prioritizing the dimensions of service quality, International Journal of Service Industry Management, Vol 5, No. 4, pp. 39-52.

Rossiter, J. R. (2002). The C-OAR-SE procedure for scale development in marketing, International Journal of Research in Marketing, Vol. 19, pp. 305-335.

Rubin, H. I. – Rubin, R. S. (1995). Qualitative Interviewing: The Art of Hearing Data, Sage, Thousand Oaks, CA.

Ryan, C. (ed.) (2002). The Tourist Experience, Continuum, London.

Ryan, C. (2003). Recreational Tourism: Demand and Impacts, Channell View Publication, Clevedon.

Ryan, C. – Birks, S. (2000). Passengers at Hamilton Airport, Unpublished Report for Hamilton International Airport, University of Waikato, Hamilton. In Uriely, N. (2005). The Tourist Experience: Conceptual Developments, Annals of Tourism Research, Vol. 32, No. 1, pp. 199-216.

Sanchez-Fernandez, R. – Iniesta-Bonillo, M.A. (2007). The Concept of Perceived Value: A Systematic Review of the Research, Marketing Theory, Vol. 7, No. 4, pp. 427–451.

Schau, H. J. – Muniz, A. M. , Jr – Arnould, E. J. (2009). How Brand Community Practices Create Value, Journal of Marketing, Vol. 73, September, pp. 30-51.

Schmitt, B. H. (1999). Experiential Marketing: How to Get Customers to Sense, Feel, Think, Act and Relate to Your Company and Brands, Free Press, New York.

Schmitt, B. H. (2003). Customer Experience Management: A Revolutionary Approach to Connecting with Your Customer, Wiley and Sons, New Jersey.

Schmitt, B. T. – Simonson, A. (1997). Marketing Aesthetics: The Strategic Management of Brands, Identity and Image, Free Press, New York.

Scitovsky, T. (1976). The Joyless Economy. Oxford University Press, Oxford. In In M. Morgan – J. Elbe – J. de Esteban Curiel (2009). Has the experience economy arrived? The views of destination managers in three visitor-dependent areas, International Journal of Tourism Research, Vol. 11, pp. 201–216.

Selstad, L. (2007). The social anthropology of the tourist experience: Exploring the "Middle Role", Scandinavian Journal of Hospitality and Tourism, Vol. 7, No. 1, pp. 19-33.

Shaw, C. – Ivens, J. (2005). Building Great Customer Experiences, MacMillan, New York.

Sherry, J., Jr – Kozinets, R. – Borghini, S. (2007). Agents in Paradise: Experiential Co-creation though Emplacement, Ritualization and Community, In A. Caru – B. Cova (eds.) Consumption Experience, Routledge, Oxon, pp. 17-33.

Small, J. (2008). The absence of childhood in tourism studies, Annals of Tourism Research, Vol. 35, No. 3, pp. 772-789.

Smith, S. – Wheeler, J. (2002). Managing the Customer Experience, Prentice Hall, London.

Smith, V. (1978). Hosts and Guests, Blackwells, Oxford.

Stamboulis, Y. – Skayannis, P. (2003). Innovation strategies and technology for experienced-based tourism, Tourism Management, Vol. 24, No. 1, pp. 35-43.

Stebbins, R. A. (2007). Serious Leisure: A Perspective for Our Time, Transaction Publisher, Edison, NJ. In M. Morgan – J. Elbe – J. de Esteban Curiel (2009). Has the experience economy arrived? The views of destination managers in three visitor-dependent areas, International Journal of Tourism Research, Vol. 11, pp. 201–216.

Sternberg, E. (1997). The Iconography of the Tourism Experience, Annals of Tourism Research, Vol. 24 No. 4, pp. 951–969.

Sundbo, J. (2009). Innovation in the experience economy: a taxonomy of innovation organisations, The Service Industries Journal, Vol. 29, No. 3-4, pp. 431-455.

Suvantola, J. (2002). Tourist's Experience of Place. Ashgate, Farnham, Surrey. In M. Morgan – J. Elbe – J. de Esteban Curiel (2009). Has the experience economy arrived? The views of destination managers in three visitor-dependent areas, International Journal of Tourism Research, Vol. 11, pp. 201–216.

Swarbrooke, J. – Horner, S. (1999). Consumer Behavior in Tourism, Elsevier Butterworth-Heinemann, Burlington.

Toffler, A. (1970). Future Shock, Bantam Books, New York.

Tsai, S. (2005). Integrated marketing as management of holistic consumer experience, Business Horizons, Vol. 48, pp. 431–441.

Uriely, N. (2005). The Tourist Experience: Conceptual Developments, Annals of Tourism Research, Vol. 32, No. 1, pp. 199-216.

Urry, J. (1990). The Tourist Gaze: Leisure and Travel in Contemporary Societies, Sage, London.

Vargo, S. L. – Lusch, R. F. (2004). Evolving to a New Dominant Logic for Marketing, Journal of Marketing, Vol. 68, January, pp. 1-17.

Vargo, S. L. – Lusch, R. F. (2008). Service-Dominant Logic: Continuing the Evolution, Journal of the Academy of Marketing Science, Vol. 36, No. 1, pp. 1-10.

Volo, S. (2005). Tourism destination innovativeness. In P. Keller – T. Bieger (eds.), AIEST 55th Congress: Innovation in Tourism – Creating customer value, Assiciation Internationale d'Experts Scientifique du Tourisme, St. Gallen, Switzerlan, Vol. 47, pp. 199-211.

Volo, S. (2009). Conceptualizing Experience: A Tourist Based Approach, Journal of Hospitality Marketing & Management, Vol. 18, No. 2, pp. 111-126.

Walls, A. R. – Okumus, F. – Wang, Y. – Kwun, D. J. (2011). An epistemological view of consumer experiences. International Journal of Hospitality Management, Vol. 30, No. 1, pp. 10–21.

Wang, N. (1999). Rethinking authenticity in tourism experience, Annals of Tourism Research, Vol. 26, pp. 349–370.

Wikstrom, S. (1996). The Customer as Co-producer, European Journal of Marketing, Vol. 30, No. 4, pp. 6–19.

Williams, A. (2006). Tourism and hospitality marketing: fantasy, feeling and fun, International Journal of Contemporary Hospitality Management, Vol. 18, No. 6, pp. 482–495.

Wirtz, D. – Kruger, J. – Scollon, C. N. – Diener, E. (2003). What to do on spring break? The role of predicted, on-line, and remembered experience in future choice, Psychological Science, Vol. 14, pp. 520–524.

Woodruff, R.B. – Flint, D.J. (2006). Marketing's Service-dominant Logic and Customer Value', In R. F. Lusch and S. L. Vargo (eds.) The Service-Dominant Logic of Marketing: Dialog, Debate and Direction, pp. 183–195. M. E. Sharpe, Armonk, New York.

Wright, R. K. (2010). 'Been There, Done That': Embracing our Post-trip Experiential Recollections through the Social Construction and Subjective Consumption of Personal Narratives. In M. Morgan – P. Lugosi – J.R.B. Ritchie (eds.) The Tourism and Leisure Experience: Consumer and Managerial Perspectives, Channel View Publications, Bristol, pp. 117-136.

APPENDIX

SMALL GROUP TOURS (own pictures, 2013)

Picture 1: Free Budapest Tours: telling a legend

Picture 2: Discover Budapest tour by segway

Picture 3: Budabike - a stop at a tourist attraction

Picture 4: Free Budapest Tours: Tour in the hot downtown

Picture 5: Ghost tour in the downtown of Pest

Picture 6: Small group, more attention

BIG GROUP TOURS

Picture 8: RiverRide – the moment of splash

http://www.audiogids.lv/assets/uploads/riverride.jpg

Picture 7: RiverRide from inside – live guiding

(own picture, 2013)

Picture 9: Hop On Hop Off with audioguide,

taking pictures from the bus

http://i1.ytimg.com/vi/cl6eNzRHSNY/maxresdefault.jpg

Picture 10: The tour of Program Centrum

http://img1.indafoto.hu

ALTERNATIVE TOURS (own pictures, 2013)

Picture 11: BUPAP – Street art tour   Picture 12: When locked gates open

Picture 13 and 14: Imagine Budapest tour – the guide shows old documents and pictures

THE RESULT OF SCALE DEVELOPMENT BEFORE QUESTIONNAIRE DESIGN

Interaction
I got enough information about this tour in advance
I received clear information during the tour
The guiding was interesting / uninteresting
The guiding was involving / uninvolving
The guiding was passionate / dull
The guiding was entertaining / not entertaining
The guiding was informative / not informative
guiding was one side communication / interactive
I had no / rich interaction with the guide

Experience environment
I liked the content of the tour
The sights were visually attractive
I could hear the guiding properly
The technology in use on the tour were just the right tools
I am satisfied with the quality of the transport
I am satisfied with the weather during the tour
The schedule (timing) of the tour was precise
I felt (physically) comfortable during the tour
The tour was (physically) tiring
I felt secure during the tour

Customization
The program/guide did not leave enough time when stopping at certain sights
The tour could be more customized to my needs
The tour contained spontaneous elements
I felt I had a chance of choice during the tour
I felt I have control over my experience

Involvement
Emotional involvement

The tour was enjoyable / unenjoyable
The tour was exciting / boring
The tour was engaging / not engaging
The tour was surprising / was not surprising
The tour was inspiring / not inspiring

Mental involvement
I learned a lot during the tour / I did not learn during the tour
The tour was thought provoking / not thought provoking
The tour made me want to learn more / did not made me want to learn more
The tour was interesting / uninteresting

Social involvement
I did / did not enjoy the company of other tourists in the group
The tour had a good / bad group atmosphere
The group interaction was poor / the group interacted well with each other
I enjoyed / did not enjoy the company of my partner/family/friend(s)
I had no interaction with the guide / I had rich interaction with the guide
I did talk to locals

Flow
The tour made me lost my sense of time / I was looking at my watch often
The tour made me feel active/ passive
I lost myself in the story / I was barely listening to the guiding
The tour meant a lot to me / meant nothing to me
The tour helped me to get away from it all / did not make me get rid of my everyday thoughts

Authenticity
Most of the sights seemed authentic (genuine)
The tour was a good reflection of local life and culture
My experience seemed to be authentic
The guiding was trustworthy / doubtful
The tour was unique / not unique at all
I experienced something which I could relate to
I learnt about myself during the tour
I felt a spontaneous instance of self-discovery
I felt it contributed to my personal development

Memorability
I will have wonderful memories about this tour
I will remember many positive things about this tour
I won't forget my experience at this tour

Date:

Dear Guests! Please evaluate the sightseeing tour you are (were) taking!

1. What was the reason that you decided to choose this tour? *(You can choose more options!)*

a) it is a good value for money
b) it can be customized to my needs
c) I can visit all the major attractions in a short time
d) I can learn interesting things about the city
e) recommendation of a friend
f) online recommendation (e.g. Trip Advisor)
g) recommendation of the hotel staff
h) the theme of the tour

i) the tour was included in the trip package
j) previous experience with the same type of tour
k) previous experience with the same tour provider
l) I was not the one who chose this tour
m) the kind sales person
n) mode of transport used during tour
p) other

2. Please evaluate the **tour GUIDING performance (performance of the tour guide)** according to the pair of characteristics! To what extent is it rather „A" or „B"? Indicate your answer with „X" in each line! **The tour GUIDING performance was** .....

„A"	1	2	3	4 decidedly neutral	5	6	7	„B"	I do not know
boring								interesting	
uninvolving								involving	
dull								passionate	
one side communication								interactive	
not informative								informative	
not entertaining								entertaining	
doubtful (information)								trustworthy (information)	

3. Please evaluate the **TOUR** according to the pair of characteristics! To what extent is it rather „A" or „B"? Indicate your answer with „X" in each line! The tour (was)...

„A"	1	2	3	4 decidedly neutral	5	6	7	„B"	I do not know	N/A
unenjoyable								enjoyable		
unexciting								exciting		
not inspiring								inspiring		
not engaging								engaging		
not surprising								surprising		
I did not learn during the tour								I learned a lot		
not thought provoking								thought provoking		
boring								interesting		
did not made me want to learn more								made me want to learn more		
the sights were not visually attractive								visually attractive		
the music did not make a difference								the music I heard was uplifting		
not unique at all								unique		
worthless to me								valuable to me		
meant nothing to me								meant a lot to me		
did not make me get rid of everyday thoughts								helped me to get away from it all		
made me feel passive								made me feel active		
I was barely listening to the guiding								I lost myself in the story		
I was often looking at my watch								made me lost my sense of time		
I did not enjoy the company of others								I enjoyed the company of others in group		
bad group athmosphere								good group athmosphere		
the group interaction was poor								the group interacted well with each other		
I didnot enjoy the company of my friend/family								I enjoyed the company of my friend/family		
I had no interaction with the guide								I had rich interaction with the guide		

4. Did you do any activity during the tour? What? How did it influence your experience? *(1=not at all 2=quite not 3=slightly not 4=decidedly neutral 5=slightly yes 6=quite yes 7=completely)* Please indicate your answer with „X"!

	Did you do it?		How did it influence your experience?						
Shopping	YES	NO	1	2	3	4	5	6	7
Talking to local(s)	YES	NO	1	2	3	4	5	6	7
Eating / drinking	YES	NO	1	2	3	4	5	6	7
Other	YES		1	2	3	4	5	6	7

5. Did any smell, sights etc. catch your attention during the tour? What? How did it influence your experience? *(1=not at all 2=quite not 3=slightly not 4=decidedly neutral 5=slightly yes 6=quite yes 7=completely)* Please indicate your answer with „X"!

What?	1	2	3	4	5	6	7

*To be continued on the 2nd page...

6. How do you feel about the tour? *Indicate your answer with ,X' in each line! How much do you agree with the followings?*
(1=not at all 2=quite not 3=slightly not 4=decidedly neutral 5=slightly yes 6=quite yes 7=completely)

	1	2	3	4	5	6	7	I do not know
I got enough information about this tour in advance								
I received clear information (orientation) during the tour								
I liked the content of the tour								
I could hear the guiding properly								
The technology in use on the tour were just the right tools								
I am satisfied with the quality of the transport								
I am satisfied with the weather during the tour								
The schedule (timing) of the tour was precise								
I felt secure during the tour								
I felt (physically) comfortable during the tour								
The tour was physically tiring								
The tour provider company did its best to improve my tour experience								
The tour guide looked after me well								

	1	2	3	4	5	6	7	I do not know
Most of the sights seemed authentic / genuine								
The tour was a good reflection of local life and culture								
My experience seemed to be authentic								
I experienced something which I could relate to								
It contributed to my personal developement								
I learned about myself during the tour								
The program/guide did not leave enough time when stopping at certain sights								
The tour could be more customized to my needs								
The tour contained spontanous program elements								
I felt I had a chance of choice during the tour								
I felt the I have control over my experience								
I will have wonderful memories about this tour								
I will remember many positive things about this tour								
I will not forget my experience at this tour								

7. Please evaluate your **complete experience from the tour** according to the parameters and their pair of indicators! To what extent is it rather ,A' or ,B'? *Indicate your answer with ,X' in each line!*

	„A"	1	2	3	decidedly neutral (4)	5	6	7	„B"	I do not know
My experience from the tour was	poor								excellent	
Based on my expectations the tour was	worse								better than expected	
To what extent is the tour a good value for money?	not at all								completely	
I was satisfied with the guiding /guide	not at all								completely	
I was satisfied with the tour provider company	not at all								completely	
I was satisfied with the sights I have seen or visited	not at all								completely	
Overall, I was ____ with the tour	very dissatisfied								very satisfied	

8. What has become **the most memorable experience** from the tour? (for example: a moment, certain story or sight)

....

9. What is your nationality? .... **10. What is your gender?** a) Male b) Female

11. What is your age? a) 18 – 25 b) 26 – 35 c) 36– 45 d) 46-55 e) 56-65 f) 66 and more

12. What is your highest education? a) elementary b) high school c) university studies in process d) university

13. How many times have you been in Budapest before? .... **14. How many days do you spend in Budapest?** ....

15. To what extent were the questions and answers in the questionnarie clear for you to understand?
(1= not at all 4= I understood the half of it. 7=absolutely) | 1 | 2 | 3 | 4 | 5 | 6 | 7 |

16. Where did you order / buy this tour?
a) from a sales person on the street
b) at hotel reception
c) directly from the tour provider
d) online
e) it was included in the trip package (e.g. Budapest Card)
f) other

17. Your email address (*only for the purpose of the research*) ....

Dear Guests! Please evaluate the sightseeing tour (both by bus and ship)
you are taking with this Hop On Hop Off company!

1. What was the reason that you decided to choose this tour? *(You can choose more options!)*

a) it is a good value for money
b) it can be customized to my needs
c) I can visit all the major attractions in a short time
d) I can learn interesting things about the city
e) recommendation of a friend
f) online recommendatadation (e.g. Trip Advisor)
g) recommendation of the hotel staff
h) the theme of the tour
i) the tour was included in the trip package
j) previous experience with the same type of tour
k) previous experience with the same tour provider
l) I was not the one who chose this tour
m) the kind sales person
n) mode of transport used during tour
o) other

2. Please evaluate the tour GUIDING performance according to the pair of characteristics! To what extent is it rather „A" or „B"?
Indicate your answer with „X" in each line! **The tour GUIDING performance was ......**

„A"	1	2	3	4 decidedly neutral	5	6	7	„B"	I do not know
boring								interesting	
uninvolving								involving	
dull								passionate	
not informative								informative	
not entertaining								entertaining	
doubtful (information)								trustworthy (information)	

3. Please evaluate the TOUR according to the pair of characteristics! To what extent is it rather „A" or „B"? Indicate your answer with
„X" in each line! **The tour (was)...**

„A"	1	2	3	4 decidedly neutral	5	6	7	„B"	I do not know	N/A
unenjoyable								enjoyable		
unexciting								exciting		
not inspiring								inspiring		
not engaging								engaging		
not surprising								surprising		
I did not learn during the tour								I learned a lot		
not thought provoking								thought provoking		
boring								interesting		
did not made me want to learn more								made me want to learn more		
the sights were not visually attractive								visually attractive		
the music did not make a difference								the music I heard was uplifting		
not unique at all								unique		
worthless to me								valuable to me		
meant nothing to me								meant a lot to me		
did not make me get rid of everyday thoughts								helped me to get away from it all		
made me feel passive								made me feel active		
I was barely listening to the guiding								I lost myself in the story		
I was often looking at my watch								made me lost my sense of time		
I did not enjoy the company of others in group								I enjoyed the company of others in group		
bad group atmosphere								good group athmosphere		
the group interaction was poor								the group interacted well with each other		
I didnot enjoy the company of my friend/family								I enjoyed the company of my friend/family		
I had no interaction with the host-ess								I had rich interaction with the host-ess		

4. Did you do any activity during the tour? What? How did it influence your experience? *(1=not at all, 2=quite not, 3=slightly not, 4=decidedly neutral, 5=slightly yes, 6=quite yes, 7=completely) Please, indicate your answer with „X"!*

	Did you do it?		How did it influence your experience?						
Shopping	YES	NO	1	2	3	4	5	6	7
Talking to local(s)	YES	NO	1	2	3	4	5	6	7
Eating / drinking	YES	NO	1	2	3	4	5	6	7
Other	YES		1	2	3	4	5	6	7

5. Did any smell, sights etc. catch your attention during the tour? What? How did it influence your experience? *(1=not at all, 2=quite not, 3=slightly not, 4=decidedly neutral, 5=slightly yes, 6=quite yes, 7=completely)Please, indicate your answer with „X"!*

What?	1	2	3	4	5	6	7

*To be continued on the 2nd page.

6. How do you feel about the tour? *Indicate your answer with „X" in each line! How much do you agree with the followings?*
(1=not at all, 2=quite not, 3=slightly not, 4=decidedly neutral, 5=slightly yes, 6=quite yes, 7=completely)

	1	2	3	4	5	6	7	I do not know
I got enough information about this tour in advance								
I received clear information (orientation) during the tour								
I liked the content of the tour								
I could hear the guiding properly								
The technology in use on the tour were just the right tools								
I am satisfied with the quality of the transport								
I am satisfied with the weather during the tour								
The schedule (timing) of the tour was precise								
I felt secure during the tour								
I felt (physically) comfortable during the tour								
The tour was physically tiring								
The tour provider company did its best to improve my tour experience								
The tour guide / host-ess looked after me well								

	1	2	3	4	5	6	7	I do not know
Most of the sights seemed authentic / genuine								
The tour was a good reflection of local life and culture								
My experience seemed to be authentic								
I experienced something which I could relate to								
It contributed to my personal developement								
I learned about myself during the tour								
The program/guide did not leave enough time when stopping at certain sights								
The tour could be more customized to my needs								
The tour contained spontanous program elements								
I felt I had a chance of choice during the tour								
I felt I have control over my experience								
I will have wonderful memories about this tour								
I will remember many positive things about this tour								
I will not forget my experience at this tour								

7. Please evaluate your **complete experience** from the tour according to the parameters and their pair of indicators! To what extent is it rather „A" or „B"? *Indicate your answer with „X" in each line!*

	„A"	1	2	3	decidedly neutral (4)	5	6	7	„B"	I do not know
My experience from the tour was	poor								excellent	
Based on my expectations the tour was	worse								better than expected	
To what extent is the tour a good value for money?	not at all								completely	
I was satisfied with the guiding /guide	not at all								completely	
I was satisfied with the tour provider company	not at all								completely	
I was satisfied with the sights I have seen or visited	not at all								completely	
Overall, I was ____ with the tour	very dissatisfied								very satisfied	

8. What has become **the most memorable experience** from the tour? (for example: a certain story or a sight)

_____

9. What is your nationality? _____   10. What is your gender?   a) Male   b) Female

11. What is your age?   a) 18 – 25   b) 26 – 35   c) 36 – 45   d) 46 – 55   e) 56 – 65   f) 66 and more

12. What is your highest education?   a) elementary   b) high school   c) university studies in process   d) university

13. How many times have you been in Budapest before? _____   14. How many days do you spend in Budapest? _____

15. To what extent were the questions and answers in the questionnarie clear for you to understand?
(1= not at all, 4= I understood the half of it, 7=absolutely)

1	2	3	4	5	6	7

16. Where did you buy this tour?
a) from a sales person on the street
b) at hotel reception
f) other
d) online
e) it was included in the trip package (e.g. Budapest Card)

17. Your email address *("only for the purpose of the research)* _____

FREQUENCIES – BIG GROUP TOURS SAMPLE

Gender

		Frequency	Percent	Valid Percent	Cumulative Percent
Valid	Male	66	46,8	55,5	55,5
	Female	53	37,6	44,5	100,0
	Total	119	84,4	100,0	
Missing	8	22	15,6		
Total		141	100,0		

Age

		Frequency	Percent	Valid Percent	Cumulative Percent
Valid	18-25	34	24,1	26,4	26,4
	26-35	40	28,4	31,0	57,4
	36-45	24	17,0	18,6	76,0
	46-55	20	14,2	15,5	91,5
	56-65	7	5,0	5,4	96,9
	66+	4	2,8	3,1	100,0
	Total	129	91,5	100,0	
Missing	8	12	8,5		
Total		141	100,0		

Nation

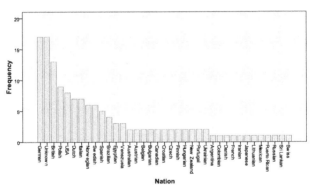

Nation

Nation

		Frequency	Percent	Valid Percent	Cumulative Percent
Valid	German	17	12,1	12,1	12,1
	Unknown	17	12,1	12,1	24,1
	British	13	9,2	9,2	33,3
	Polish	9	6,4	6,4	39,7
	USA	8	5,7	5,7	45,4
	Dutch	7	5,0	5,0	50,4
	Italian	7	5,0	5,0	55,3
	Norwegian	6	4,3	4,3	59,6
	Swedish	6	4,3	4,3	63,8
	Spanish	5	3,5	3,5	67,4
	Brazilian	4	2,8	2,8	70,2
	Egyptian	3	2,1	2,1	72,3
	Venezuela	3	2,1	2,1	74,5
	Australian	2	1,4	1,4	75,9
	Austrian	2	1,4	1,4	77,3
	Belgian	2	1,4	1,4	78,7
	Bulgarian	2	1,4	1,4	80,1
	Canadian	2	1,4	1,4	81,6
	Croatian	2	1,4	1,4	83,0
	Czech	2	1,4	1,4	84,4
	Finnish	2	1,4	1,4	85,8
	Hungarian	2	1,4	1,4	87,2
	New Zealand	2	1,4	1,4	88,7
	Portugal	2	1,4	1,4	90,1
	Ukrainian	2	1,4	1,4	91,5
	Argentina	1	,7	,7	92,2
	Colombian	1	,7	,7	92,9
	Danish	1	,7	,7	93,6
	French	1	,7	,7	94,3
	Iranian	1	,7	,7	95,0
	Japanese	1	,7	,7	95,7
	Lithuanian	1	,7	,7	96,5
	Mexican	1	,7	,7	97,2
	Puerto Rican	1	,7	,7	97,9
	Russian	1	,7	,7	98,6
	Sri Lankan	1	,7	,7	99,3
	Swiss	1	,7	,7	100,0
	Total	141	100,0	100,0	

FREQUENCIES – SMALL GROUP TOURS SAMPLE

Gender

		Frequency	Percent	Valid Percent	Cumulative Percent
Valid	Male	56	47,5	51,4	51,4
	Female	53	44,9	48,6	100,0
	Total	109	92,4	100,0	
Missing	8	9	7,6		
Total		118	100,0		

Gender

		Frequency	Percent	Valid Percent	Cumulative Percent
Valid	Male	56	47,5	51,4	51,4
	Female	53	44,9	48,6	100,0
	Total	109	92,4	100,0	
Missing	8	9	7,6		
Total		118	100,0		

Nation

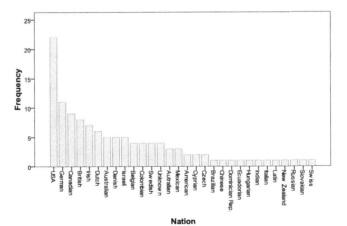

Nation

Nation

		Frequency	Percent	Valid Percent	Cumulative Percent
Valid	USA	22	18,6	18,6	18,6
	German	11	9,3	9,3	28,0
	Canadian	9	7,6	7,6	35,6
	British	8	6,8	6,8	42,4
	Irish	7	5,9	5,9	48,3
	Dutch	6	5,1	5,1	53,4
	Australian	5	4,2	4,2	57,6
	Danish	5	4,2	4,2	61,9
	Israeli	5	4,2	4,2	66,1
	Belgian	4	3,4	3,4	69,5
	Colombian	4	3,4	3,4	72,9
	Swedish	4	3,4	3,4	76,3
	Unknown	4	3,4	3,4	79,7
	Autralian	3	2,5	2,5	82,2
	Mexican	3	2,5	2,5	84,7
	American	2	1,7	1,7	86,4
	Cyprian	2	1,7	1,7	88,1
	Czech	2	1,7	1,7	89,8
	Brazilian	1	,8	,8	90,7
	Chinese	1	,8	,8	91,5
	Dominician Rep.	1	,8	,8	92,4
	Ecuadorian	1	,8	,8	93,2
	Hungarian	1	,8	,8	94,1
	Indian	1	,8	,8	94,9
	Italian	1	,8	,8	95,8
	Latin	1	,8	,8	96,6
	New Zealand	1	,8	,8	97,5
	Russian	1	,8	,8	98,3
	Slovakian	1	,8	,8	99,2
	Swiss	1	,8	,8	100,0
	Total	118	100,0	100,0	

FREQUENCIES – ALTERNATIVE TOURS SAMPLE

Gender

		Frequency	Percent	Valid Percent	Cumulative Percent
Valid	Female	69	77,5	82,1	82,1
	Male	15	16,9	17,9	100,0
	Total	84	94,4	100,0	
Missing	8	5	5,6		
Total		89	100,0		

Age

		Frequency	Percent	Valid Percent	Cumulative Percent
Valid	18-25	14	15,7	15,7	15,7
	26-35	30	33,7	33,7	49,4
	36-45	21	23,6	23,6	73,0
	46-55	9	10,1	10,1	83,1
	56-65	8	9,0	9,0	92,1
	66+	7	7,9	7,9	100,0
	Total	89	100,0	100,0	

Home city

		Frequency	Percent	Valid Percent	Cumulative Percent
Valid	Budapest	75	84,3	84,3	84,3
	Unknown	5	5,6	5,6	89,9
	Halásztelek	2	2,2	2,2	92,1
	Szentendre	2	2,2	2,2	94,4
	Budapest/Párizs	1	1,1	1,1	95,5
	Göd	1	1,1	1,1	96,6
	Gödöllő	1	1,1	1,1	97,8
	Kecskemét	1	1,1	1,1	98,9
	Törökbálint	1	1,1	1,1	100,0
	Total	89	100,0	100,0	

RESULTS OF PRINCIPAL COMPONENT ANALYSIS (PCA) – SPSS 20.0

Independent Variables

Rotated Component Matrix[a]

	Component			
	1	2	3	4
interest2		,194	,271	,086
involv2		,157	,294	,234
passion2		,109	,309	,230
infomtv2		,168	,055	,100
entert2		,142	,284	,141
trustw2		,331	-,035	,052
durinfo6	,312	,248		,083
content6	,343	,256		,132
hear6	,109	,293		,082
transp6	,143		,374	,132
schedu6	,203		,116	,033
secur6	,251		,294	,017
comfort6	,181		,159	,131
sponta6	,204	,073	-,021	
choice6	,127	,080	,069	
control6	,114	,076	,227	

Extraction Method: Principal Component Analysis.
a. Rotation converged in 6 iterations.

Communalities

	Initial	Extraction
interest2	1,000	,721
involv2	1,000	,643
passion2	1,000	,716
infomtv2	1,000	,731
entert2	1,000	,766
trustw2	1,000	,672
durinfo6	1,000	,752
content6	1,000	,738
hear6	1,000	,647
transp6	1,000	,642
schedu6	1,000	,555
secur6	1,000	,775
comfort6	1,000	,725
sponta6	1,000	,671
choice6	1,000	,833
control6	1,000	,747

Extraction Method: Principal

Total Variance Explained

Compone nt	Initial Eigenvalues			Loadings			Loadings		
	Total	% of Variance	Cumulativ e %	Total	% of Variance	Cumulativ e %	Total	% of Variance	Cumulativ e %
1	6,838	42,739	42,739	6,838	42,739	42,739	3,984	24,901	24,901
2	1,910	11,936	54,674	1,910	11,936	54,674	2,700	16,877	41,778
3	1,594	9,965	64,639	1,594	9,965	64,639	2,328	14,553	56,331
4	,992	6,198	70,837	,992	6,198	70,837	2,321	14,506	70,837
5	,652	4,075	74,913						
6	,593	3,705	78,618						
7	,535	3,344	81,962						
8	,472	2,950	84,912						
9	,425	2,654	87,566						
10	,379	2,371	89,937						
11	,337	2,109	92,046						
12	,299	1,871	93,917						
13	,286	1,787	95,704						
14	,247	1,545	97,249						
15	,229	1,430	98,679						
16	,211	1,321	100,000						

Extraction Method: Principal Component Analysis.

PCA (SPPSS 20.0) – experience-involvement

	Component		
	1	2	3
enjoy3		,098	,210
excit3		,345	,090
inspir3		,432	,261
engag3		,395	,304
surpr3		,357	,282
learn3		,379	,106
thoupro3		,429	,292
intere3		,323	,213
morelea3		,459	,208
visuatt3		,123	,185
uniq3	,441		,154
valuea3	,468		,032
meaninf3	,397		,204
getway3	,163		,254
active3	,299		,383
loststor3	,204		,195
compot3	,229	,123	
gratmos3	,317	,184	
grintera3	,168	,182	
intergui3	,122	,340	

Extraction Method: Principal Component

Communalities

	Initial	Extraction
enjoy3	1,000	,560
excit3	1,000	,654
inspir3	1,000	,632
engag3	1,000	,637
surpr3	1,000	,499
learn3	1,000	,636
thoupro3	1,000	,485
intere3	1,000	,664
morelea3	1,000	,540
visuatt3	1,000	,458
uniq3	1,000	,555
valuea3	1,000	,751
meaninf3	1,000	,684
getway3	1,000	,637
active3	1,000	,673
loststor3	1,000	,553
compot3	1,000	,791
gratmos3	1,000	,711
grintera3	1,000	,780
intergui3	1,000	,531

Extraction Method: Principal

Total Variance Explained

Compone nt	Initial Eigenvalues			Loadings			Loadings		
	Total	% of Variance	Cumulativ e %	Total	% of Variance	Cumulativ e %	Total	% of Variance	Cumulativ e %
1	9,711	48,554	48,554	9,711	48,554	48,554	4,083	20,415	20,415
2	1,680	8,398	56,952	1,680	8,398	56,952	3,285	16,423	36,838
3	1,041	5,203	62,155	1,041	5,203	62,155	3,073	15,367	52,205
4	,909	4,543	66,699	,909	4,543	66,699	2,899	14,494	66,699
5	,824	4,122	70,821						
6	,685	3,426	74,247						
7	,663	3,314	77,561						
8	,627	3,136	80,698						
9	,489	2,444	83,142						
10	,467	2,334	85,476						
11	,432	2,158	87,634						
12	,370	1,851	89,485						
13	,333	1,667	91,152						
14	,324	1,619	92,771						
15	,310	1,551	94,322						
16	,277	1,385	95,708						
17	,270	1,348	97,056						
18	,234	1,172	98,228						
19	,197	,986	99,214						
20	,157	,786	100,000						

Extraction Method: Principal Component Analysis.

PCA (SPSS 20.0) – experience outcome variables

Rotated Component Matrix[a]

	Component		
	1	2	3
sighaut6		,346	-,090
reflocal6		,181	,269
expaut6		,292	,249
relate6	,529	,216	
persdev6	,357	,093	
leamysf6	-,025	,228	
memo6	,251		,114
remem6	,372		,190
forget6	,183		,227

Extraction Method: Principal Component Analysis.
a. Rotation converged in 5 iterations.

Communalities

	Initial	Extraction
sighaut6	1,000	,734
reflocal6	1,000	,795
expaut6	1,000	,789
relate6	1,000	,655
persdev6	1,000	,724
leamysf6	1,000	,733
memo6	1,000	,820
remem6	1,000	,884
forget6	1,000	,778

Extraction Method: Principal Component Analysis.

Total Variance Explained

Compone nt	Initial Eigenvalues			Loadings			Loadings		
	Total	% of Variance	Cumulativ e %	Total	% of Variance	Cumulativ e %	Total	% of Variance	Cumulativ e %
1	4,710	52,335	52,335	4,710	52,335	52,335	2,629	29,210	29,210
2	1,169	12,987	65,322	1,169	12,987	65,322	2,492	27,684	56,893
3	1,034	11,486	76,808	1,034	11,486	76,808	1,792	19,914	76,808
4	,555	6,164	82,972						
5	,421	4,680	87,652						
6	,399	4,436	92,087						
7	,313	3,474	95,561						
8	,242	2,686	98,247						
9	,158	1,753	100,000						

Extraction Method: Principal Component Analysis.

DESCRIPTIVE STATISTICS AND BIVARIANT CORRELATIONS

Total sample

All	Cr-A	CR	AVE	Aut	CoAut	Cust	Emo EI	ExAut	Org EE	Flow EI	Intera	EI	Memo	Ment EI	Soc EI	Int EE
Authenticity*	0,8303	0,8783	0,5522	1												
Cons. Authenticity	0,8483	0,9082	0,7677	0,9108	1											
Customization	0,8238	0,8954	0,7408	0,4197	0,333	1										
Emotional EI	0,8642	0,9026	0,6505	0,6081	0,5793	0,3977	1									
Exp. Authenticity	0,717	0,8396	0,6378	0,8609	0,5742	0,4209	0,4913	1								
Organizational Exp. Envi.	0,8293	0,887	0,6638	0,5361	0,5566	0,2452	0,4799	0,3768	1							
Flow EI	0,8505	0,8933	0,6267	0,6437	0,5578	0,3845	0,7551	0,5882	0,454	1						
Interaction	0,906	0,9275	0,6812	0,5815	0,5623	0,3726	0,751	0,4594	0,5119	0,6604	1					
Experience-Involvement (EI)*	0,9382	0,9452	0,4911	0,6784	0,6105	0,4764	0,9092	0,592	0,5141	0,9002	0,7663	1				
Memorability	0,8932	0,9335	0,8242	0,6174	0,5874	0,4812	0,6408	0,4992	0,5437	0,5828	0,6586	0,6763	1			
Mental EI	0,8455	0,8963	0,6839	0,5676	0,5136	0,369	0,7583	0,4915	0,4134	0,7213	0,6378	0,8703	0,5634	1		
Social EI	0,8616	0,9065	0,7086	0,4914	0,4217	0,5091	0,5482	0,4538	0,407	0,5752	0,5566	0,7405	0,5188	0,5051	1	
Interactive Exp. Envi.	0,8077	0,8856	0,7222	0,5927	0,6018	0,2993	0,5811	0,433	0,6095	0,5484	0,5848	0,597	0,5777	0,4595	0,4352	1

*second-order latent variable

Big group (bus) tours

Bus	Cr-A	CR	AVE	Aut	CoAut	Cust	Emo EI	ExAut	Org EE	Flow EI	Intera	EI	Memo	Ment EI	Soc EI	Int EE
Authenticity*	0,823	0,8737	0,5417	1												
Cons. Authenticity	0,8554	0,9121	0,7763	0,8893	1											
Customization	0,7436	0,8525	0,662	0,3534	0,2679	1										
Emotional EI	0,8314	0,8818	0,6001	0,6197	0,5969	0,3702	1									
Exp. Authenticity	0,7681	0,8639	0,6797	0,8391	0,4975	0,3514	0,4642	1								
Organizational Exp. Envi.	0,8477	0,898	0,6886	0,479	0,527	0,1058	0,4833	0,2818	1							
Flow EI	0,8447	0,8906	0,6215	0,5736	0,471	0,2813	0,7384	0,5262	0,376	1						
Interaction	0,8994	0,9228	0,6666	0,5307	0,5053	0,2941	0,7499	0,4046	0,4528	0,6536	1					
Experience-Involvement (EI)*	0,9248	0,9342	0,4448	0,6537	0,5831	0,3859	0,9102	0,5447	0,4722	0,8973	0,7692	1				
Memorability	0,894	0,9333	0,824	0,5951	0,5773	0,3805	0,6625	0,4401	0,5736	0,5303	0,5401	0,6698	1			
Mental EI	0,8002	0,8702	0,6273	0,5856	0,5674	0,2973	0,7585	0,4341	0,4101	0,7105	0,6765	0,8713	0,6079	1		
Social EI	0,7972	0,8683	0,6231	0,3901	0,2777	0,3821	0,4977	0,4093	0,2985	0,5171	0,4791	0,6759	0,4314	0,4427	1	
Interactive Exp. Envi.	0,7878	0,8758	0,7032	0,5296	0,5312	0,2584	0,5355	0,3716	0,5415	0,4517	0,4536	0,5187	0,6598	0,4256	0,2916	1

DESCRIPTIVE STATISTICS AND BIVARIANT VARIABLES

Small group tours

Small group	Cr-A	CR	AVE	Aut	CoAut	Cust	Emo EI	ExAut	Org EE	Flow EI	Intera	EI	Memo	Men EI	Soc EI	Int EE
Authenticity*	0,8303	0,8775	0,5476	1												
Cons. Authenticity	0,7742	0,8687	0,6894	0,918	1											
Customization	0,8947	0,9344	0,826	0,5525	0,48	1										
Emotional EI	0,9011	0,927	0,7177	0,5675	0,5178	0,4524	1									
Exp. Authenticity	0,7094	0,8375	0,6324	0,5045	0,6614	0,5277	0,514	1								
Organizational Exp. Envi.	0,7553	0,8419	0,5736	0,4231	0,4376	0,4736	0,4415	0,3269	1							
Flow EI	0,8405	0,887	0,6134	0,6472	0,5723	0,4967	0,7185	0,4006	0,6038	1						
Interaction	0,8842	0,9123	0,6359	0,4557	0,4261	0,6204	0,7252	0,5436	0,4318	0,5404	1					
Experience-Involvement (EI)*	0,9439	0,9502	0,5173	0,654	0,5736	0,5756	0,8941	0,616	0,4891	0,6654	0,688	1				
Memorability	0,9105	0,9438	0,8486	0,6133	0,5702	0,47	0,6223	0,507	0,408	0,7128	0,5499	0,7108	1			
Mental EI	0,8687	0,9104	0,7175	0,4988	0,4021	0,66	0,7707	0,5013	0,4312	0,6513	0,6154	0,8807	0,5504	1		
Social EI	0,8801	0,9187	0,7396	0,5364	0,4736		0,5357		0,407		0,4601	0,7777	0,6114	0,5617	1	
Interactive Exp. Envi.	0,7951	0,8728	0,6994	0,5213	0,5162	0,4548	0,6515	0,4266	0,5416	0,5695	0,6648	0,6594	0,5417	0,5492	0,483	1

Alternative tours

Alternative	Cr-A	CR	AVE	Aut	CoAut	Cust	Emo EI	ExAut	Org EE	Flow EI	Intera	EI	Memo	Men EI	Soc EI	Int EE
Authenticity*	0,7243	0,8161	0,4506	1												
Cons. Authenticity	0,8493	0,9087	0,7688	0,9054	1											
Customization	0,8078	0,8855	0,723	0,3005	0,2141	1										
Emotional EI	0,8421	0,8895	0,6209	0,5419	0,5052	0,2418	1									
Exp. Authenticity	0,5253	0,7464	0,5208	0,7263	0,3659	0,3136	0,3696	1								
Organizational Exp. Envi.	0,762	0,833	0,5733	0,5515	0,5127	0,1777	0,4221	0,3805	1							
Flow EI	0,8063	0,8655	0,5646	0,584	0,4655	0,2372	0,7831	0,5244	0,4477	1						
Interaction	0,8714	0,9034	0,6107	0,5699	0,55	0,2428	0,7591	0,3582	0,4313	0,6383	1					
Experience-Involvement (EI)*	0,9142	0,9263	0,4214	0,6068	0,5188	0,2844	0,9212	0,4891	0,4215	0,9068	0,7223	1				
Memorability	0,8751	0,9231	0,8	0,7438	0,6655	0,4394	0,6024	0,5543	0,686	0,5838	0,5908	0,6473	1			
Mental EI	0,8534	0,9009	0,695	0,4188	0,3278	0,2059	0,6603	0,3863	0,1568	0,6534	0,4104	0,8026	0,4518	1		
Social Invo	0,7495	0,8431	0,5782	0,4152	0,3732	0,2604	0,4676	0,3051	0,2913	0,4619	0,4878	0,6132	0,4495	0,2895	1	
Interac exp envi	0,7654	0,863	0,6785	0,5852	0,6003	0,14	0,4882	0,3095	0,6469	0,5019	0,5187	0,4894	0,4932	0,206	0,359	1

Lightning Source UK Ltd.
Milton Keynes UK
UKOW04f1844160717

305430UK00001B/114/P